THE
HIGH-POTENTIAL LEADER

How to **Grow Fast,**
Take on **New Responsibilities,**
and **Make an Impact**

RAM CHARAN
with **GERI WILLIGAN AND DEB GIFFEN**

Cover image: © mattpaul/Getty Images
Cover design: Wiley

This book is printed on acid-free paper.

Copyright © 2017 by John Wiley & Sons, Inc. All rights reserved.

Published by John Wiley & Sons, Inc., Hoboken, New Jersey
Published simultaneously in Canada

For general information about our other products and services, please contact our
Customer Care Department within the United States at (800) 762-2974, outside the
United States at (317) 572-3993 or fax (317) 572-4002.

Wiley publishes in a variety of print and electronic formats and by print-on-demand.
Some material included with standard print versions of this book may not be included
in e-books or in print-on-demand. If this book refers to media such as a CD or DVD that
is not included in the version you purchased, you may download this material at http://
booksupport.wiley.com. For more information about Wiley products, visit www.wiley.com.

**Library of Congress Cataloging-in-Publication Data has been applied for and is on file
with the Library of Congress.**

978-1-119-28695-0 (hardback)
978-1-119-28707-0 (ePDF)
978-1-119-28706-3(ePUB)

Printed in the United States of America

10 9 8 7 6 5 4 3 2 1

What is the true value creator and competitive advantage for your company? Spotting and deploying talent. Especially in this continuously transforming economy, it is what sets one company ahead of another. This is true for born-digital companies that have become extraordinarily large and continue to expand, and for traditional companies that are waking up to the need to transform.

This book shows high-potential leaders—those who could someday lead a large organization—how to create their own paths and build the essential skills needed to live up to their great promise. At the same time, this book explains to top management, chief human resources officers, and other leadership developers how to identify their high-potential leaders and facilitate their development ahead of competition.

Contents

Dedicated to the hearts and souls of the joint family of twelve siblings and cousins living under one roof for fifty years, whose personal sacrifices made my formal education possible.

High-Potential Leaders Are Crucial to Helping Businesses Adapt and Thrive in the Digital Age

If you are one of those leaders who has high potential to lead a large, complex organization, this is your time. Companies need you. Get ready to accelerate your growth by taking charge of it. This book will show you how to build the skills and capabilities you'll need, and how and when to make big moves that will get you ready and battle test you.

If you're an HR expert charged with building your company's leadership pipeline, your job must change. You need a new approach to find and develop leaders who can deal with the immense complexity and challenges businesses face. Using this book as a guide, you will be able to redefine leadership potential and let your high-potential leaders set their own paths. The last chapter will help you rethink your role in supporting them as they drive their own exponential growth.

The Urgent Need for High-Potential Leaders

The biggest concern I hear among senior leaders today is, How can we stay relevant in this increasingly complex and fast-moving world? The truth is, some can't. They're not equipped to help their companies reinvent themselves for the new game. Nor are the leaders next in line, who've been groomed to fit the same obsolete mold.

Companies big and small are coming to realize that it will take leaders with a different way of thinking and different skills to reinvent the business. They are having to redefine the very notion of what a successful leader looks like. Now the race is on to find those with high potential to lead the company onto new paths in a world of constant change.

You've heard it before—the changes being wrought by things like digitization, algorithms, and data analytics will be as radical as the Industrial Revolution. We've already seen companies such as Facebook, Google, and Amazon cause revolutions in consumer behavior and reach the stratosphere in market value in record time. More of these are yet to come, led by people with the capacity to conceive and grow them. In a decade, the $72 trillion global economy is on a trajectory to be 50 percent greater than it is today. Products and services not yet invented will give consumers entirely different experiences and make some companies obsolete.

This is a time for leaders who can thrive in the face of relentless change, complexity, and uncertainty. Many companies have such leaders buried at lower levels. They need to find them, develop them, and find ways to use them to help the company adapt. And they need to move fast on this. "Born digital" companies are on the prowl and will gladly poach whatever high-potential talent traditional companies overlook.

High-potential leaders themselves shouldn't just sit back and wait to be discovered. They should decide for themselves whether they have what it takes to someday take a large team, business unit, function, or the whole corporation to new heights and make a plan to ready themselves to create the future.

What "High Potential" Means Now

Everyone has potential to grow, but not everyone, not even every person with leadership skills, has the potential to lead a large, complex organization in the near and distant future.

Amid everything that is new and different, today's high-potential leaders, or "hipos," must be able to identify the untapped opportunities their companies will pursue and mobilize the organization. This is a weakness in many older business leaders today. Understandably. Throughout their careers, growth was defined as improving on things that already existed: increasing profits through cost cutting, tweaking products for adjacent markets, or acquiring other companies in the same industry. More radical changes like reinventing the entire business model, reshaping the entire ecosystem of supply and distribution, or rethinking the entire customer experience have been rare in the life of a company.

It's now clear that businesses might need to be transformed more than once in a leader's tenure, and today's hipos must be prepared for that. They should exhibit three characteristics that the previous generation of leaders did not always need:

1. **They imagine on a large scale.** Hipos can take in a ton of information from many different sources and almost instantly find what could be meaningful. In doing so, they pick up clues about what might be possible, and they dream big. In the past, wild dreams or visions of things that don't yet exist might have been considered delusional, but hipos don't see it that way. If they personally lack the capability to realize the picture they have in their heads, they know they can use technology, algorithms, and other people's capabilities to make it real. They are psychologically prepared to scale it up very fast—and go after it fearlessly.

   Alphabet, now the umbrella company for Google and other subsidiaries, has a whole population of people who are working to solve the world's biggest problems. Google X, the semi-secret group charged with developing revolutionary ideas, created the driverless car and Google Glass, which is poised to take hold as a key element in the Internet of Things.

It's not just start-ups that need this kind of imagination. It's every company. Hipos have it.

2. **They seek what they need to make it happen.** I had just finished speaking to a group of executives about how to set up an advisory board when a young man approached me. "Do you have a minute?" he asked. Polite but straightforward, he continued, "I run a small company, much smaller than the corporations you're used to working with. Would you consider advising me?" It's no secret that I've worked with a lot of big, well-known companies, but he was undaunted. What I came to learn was that he had sized up his market opportunity, and it was huge. He wanted to grow his company very fast and was seeking help building the capacity for it.

   Hipos will talk to anyone. They don't just stay within the hierarchy. A young Steve Jobs didn't hesitate to call Bill Hewlett, cofounder of tech giant Hewlett-Packard, when he was seeking technical help. Pat Gallagher was young and relatively inexperienced when he was groomed to take over his family's Chicago-based insurance brokerage in 1983. Having run only the sales force, he wanted to understand what the CEO job entailed, so he reached out to the CEO of McDonnell Douglas, a company far different and much bigger than his own. The CEO took time to talk to him, and Gallagher eventually took his firm to number four in the United States. Forums like the G100 and Singularity University provide opportunities for that.

3. **They understand the concept of the ecosystem.** Companies rarely act alone in delivering their product or service. Hipos understand the complex web of participants, from the makers of small parts that go into larger ones to the mom-and-pop shops or FedEx fleet that delivers the product. Walmart became a juggernaut of low cost because of how it used its tight relationships with suppliers, the largest of which were

housed right at the Bentonville, Arkansas, headquarters. Walmart schooled its suppliers in state-of-the-art logistics that reduced inventories but kept store shelves stocked with merchandise that turned over very quickly. Both Walmart and the supplier grew, and consumers benefited from low prices.

Digital-age versions of rethinking the business ecosystem abound. Apple's iPod was a nifty device, but it became a sensation because iTunes changed the way music was packaged, priced, and distributed. Amazon thrives on algorithms that predict a customer's need and delivers it through an ecosystem of sellers, purchase options, and delivery methods.

Hipos have the ability to see the total picture, to conjure a mental image of the web of interrelationships, and to think imaginatively about how to redesign it.

Hipos will come primarily from the fifty-three million millennials in the work force now. This generation has been steeped from an early age in video, the Internet, and social media. They grew up in an information-rich world and a global social hive, interconnected and living with unprecedented social transparency. They've had instant access to vast amounts of information from around the world, conditioning their brains to rapid thinking and communication. Text messaging and Twitter train them to be brief and to the point, a sharp contrast with the belabored PowerPoint presentations the baby boomers were expected to use. With a wide mental bandwidth and ability to absorb key information, they can construct a bigger picture very quickly. All that plays to a hipo's advantage:

They adapt quickly to the new—because they've seen brands, trends, celebrities, and social conventions rise and fall overnight.

They have diverse social networks—because they're connected to people far beyond their local environment, they've traveled, and they've been exposed to a wide array of viewpoints through social media.

They have a change-the-world mentality—because they've seen unknowns become well-knowns with one viral video, and college dropouts become billionaires before they turned thirty-five. They've seen Mark Zuckerberg in a hoodie speaking to an audience of buttoned-down security analysts and Elon Musk launch SpaceX, not to mention beautiful electric cars. The success stories are known across the globe, inspiring hipos everywhere.

The qualities of today's hipos are clearly present in born digital companies, where Jeff Bezos of Amazon, Mark Zuckerberg of Facebook, Reed Hastings of Netflix, and Reid Hoffman of LinkedIn are the poster children. They also exist in established companies, in people like Jeff Immelt, CEO of GE, and Brent Saunders, CEO of Allergan. And they are found in scores of entrepreneurs who have left big companies to start their own businesses.

Not every hipo is destined to be a chief executive who creates or transforms a business; they can make huge contributions in other top positions to keep their companies at the cutting edge. Mary Anne Elliott, for example, is head of HR at Marsh, where she works closely with the CEO and CFO in a pivotal role to transform and steer the business. Bonnie Hill was an accomplished CEO and college dean and a director of several boards; at Home Depot she was instrumental in fixing the board's approach to compensation when it came under fire and rebuilding shareholder relations.

Earlier classes of hipos had the same intelligence and ambition today's hipos have, but they met different criteria. In most cases, they were picked by their immediate boss, usually because of their extraordinary and consistent performance in the existing job.

Performance was largely measured by numbers, with little digging for how the results were achieved. It helped to be good at managing upward, communicating well, and pleasing the boss by taking things off his plate.

Some basic leadership traits like high integrity and the ability to communicate are constant, and performance always matters, but they are mere table stakes. Without the qualities and abilities the fast-changing world now demands, a leader is not likely to succeed in a high-level leadership job, at least not for long.

An Important Distinction

Some people are *high-potential individuals*. Let's say you're a terrific thinker and analyst in your own specialty, or you have an exceptional talent or expertise. You do your most productive work in private, free from distractions that intrude on solving the problem at hand. When you are interrupted by a meeting or conference, you can't wait to get back to your real work.

It doesn't take deep psychological analysis to see that such people are not going to excel at leading other people. High-potential individuals would be losing ground if they set their sights on a job where they have to deal with all sorts of people and relationship issues and do the kind of strategic thinking they have little interest in. They may later develop the requisite skills or interest, at which time they could be reevaluated. But for now, they should stay with their strengths. There's no shortage of great opportunities for talented individuals.

Craig Silverstein, for example, was Sergey Brin's and Larry Page's first employee at Google. They hired him to help build their search engine while all were still at Stanford University. Not long after joining the company, he told *The Wall Street Journal* he felt he should try a managerial role. But after several months he backed away from it, having decided he "wasn't very good at it." Silverstein became Google's director of technology and stayed with the company until 2012. (He left to join another start-up, the nonprofit online Khan Academy, which aims to educate students in math, science, humanities, and finance in developing countries with scarce educational resources.)

High-potential *leaders*, on the other hand, multiply the energy and skills of others. Their value lies not in what they can personally accomplish, but in how they can bring together and motivate other people to accomplish much more than any one individual could do on their own. They *integrate* specialized expertise, differing viewpoints, and narrow interests to create new solutions and make better, faster decisions than would otherwise happen.

Getting Hipos There Faster

Hipos reach their leadership potential through the disciplined routine practice of essential skills combined with periodic leaps. Developing skills through daily, weekly, monthly practice may seem uninspiring, but many a CEO has failed because of weakness in one or two of them. Skill building, however, goes only so far. An essential part of a hipo's progress is taking *big leaps* in scope, complexity, and ambiguity. Jumping into challenging new situations not only tests the person, but it's how hipos build the higher-order skills and judgment they'll need to run a large organization today. It accelerates growth.

Mark Fields joined Ford Motor Company as one of many bright young leaders, but he pressed for jobs that others didn't want. He took a job in Argentina running sales and marketing, then became head of the Argentine unit when it was struggling. From there, he went to Mazda in Japan, which Ford had a large stake in. He inherited a dispirited team, an unfocused brand, and a financial sinkhole. Like his previous leaps, this one challenged him to diagnose what needed fixing and to get it done fast in a completely unfamiliar context. "I always choose to run to the fire," he told *The Wall Street Journal*'s Joann Lublin in March 2016.

Fields quickly determined that the way to regain lost ground at Mazda was to take a different approach to product design, to make the products distinctive from the competition's so they weren't just competing on cost-efficiency and price. To turn the company around, however, people had to work together across functions. That was easier said than done. The Japanese worked in rigid silos, and speaking up in meetings was taboo. Fields had to break the code of silence to get ideas and information flowing cross-functionally. Breaking into smaller teams and continually encouraging people to speak up eventually worked, and people rallied behind a unified plan.

Success in Japan was followed by success in Europe and North America, and when Alan Mulally retired as CEO of Ford in 2014, Mark Fields, at fifty-three, was his successor.

Despite Ford's good health, challenges abound: where and how fast to expand, which technologies to adopt, who to partner with, and how to adapt to consumer change. Success is a work in progress, but Fields is well prepared, having tested and developed his skills in team building along with his capacity to make decisive moves in complex circumstances.

Until recently, leadership development at most companies was largely ad hoc. Hipos depended heavily on their bosses to not only recognize them but also to help them grow. It's more common now for HR departments to be involved and send promising leaders to outside education programs at places like Harvard or Wharton, or to have them participate in one-week programs to teach soft skills like awareness and empathy, or to get them a mentor or coach. Many companies rotate people among geographies or divisions, often using a two-year schedule to round people out.

Some companies—J&J, Humana, Unilever, BlackRock, Marsh, and GE, to name a few—are further ahead. GE, for example, has long been at the cutting edge, and its approach continues to evolve. For decades GE held a series of annual meetings called Session C, in which the CEO, CHRO, and other business leaders identified and tracked the hipos in each of GE's businesses. People were identified based on past performance and on the higher ups' view of the person's potential to move to higher levels. Those hipos became a resource for and responsibility of the corporation's top-most leaders. Hipos were sent to GE's famous Crotonville training center and put on task forces to solve real business problems, and the big bosses got to see who they really were as they interacted with peers from across the corporation. It was not uncommon for the CEO and CHRO to reassign a hipo to an entirely different post in one of GE's other businesses, moving people from the audit function to industrial to medical, for example, depending on what kind of developmental experience they thought the person needed.

Sometimes a hipo was moved out of a business then back to a job in the old business but several levels higher. Former CEO Jack Welch is known to have moved hipos two or three steps higher in the organizational hierarchy, and he himself experienced that as a junior manager. Rigorous reviews were a constant, so people were tested for high performance and values along the way, and they were richly rewarded to stay with the company as their experiences in different countries, business units, and positions broadened them.

We know from people like Michael Dell, Mark Zuckerberg, and Bill Gates that, given the right opportunities, it's possible for high-potential leaders to expand extremely fast. Every time those high-growth companies had an expansion burst, the complexity of the leader's job increased: more employees to organize, new governmental bodies to contend with, more foreign cultures to understand, more consumers to please, all against a backdrop of ever-changing technology and competition. These leaders became household names because they kept learning, adapting, and building their skills to quickly master the complexity, create a clear path, and execute it by mobilizing others.

At most companies, the career track for hipos is slower. People move step by step, often vertically within one business function.

The development opportunities they're offered are one-size-fits-all. The next Mark Zuckerberg follows the same path at the same pace as every other leader.

Status quo leadership development programs leave companies at serious risk of coming up short when it comes time to fill the most important leadership jobs. And that time could be sooner rather than later. Even as hipos take greater control of their own growth, companies have an urgent need to change their approach to finding and growing them.

How Hipos Can Use This Book

Let's assume you meet the criteria for a hipo leader. You have ambition and there's demand for your skills, so of course you want to develop yourself as quickly as possible. Maybe your company has identified you as a high-potential leader, maybe not. Either way, you should take charge of your personal growth, because the development your company maps out for you might be too slow, and worse, might not build all the capabilities you'll need for the topmost jobs. You will likely be able to expand faster if you create your own development path.

The purpose of this book is to help you continually expand, to keep building your skills, and to define your next step or leap. I'll show you how to find opportunities and deal with the hurdles, while you double or triple your leadership capabilities and capacity every three to four years.

You can control your destiny. It used to be that information was power. But now we have the Internet and social media. It's easier than ever before to look at things from the outside in. You have a lot more access to sources of information online, and you can join networks and work on cross-industry, cross-country, cross-unit teams. You can know more, build a wider span of relationships, and learn fast, and a fast-changing world creates new opportunities for leaders every day.

Part I of this book will guide you through a series of leadership skills you should practice. It takes mindful repetition of these basic skills to master them. Just as professional athletes practice their physical skills, you need to practice the mental and emotional skills you'll use as part of the new generation of leaders. I'll explain how you can demonstrate your potential, be confident of delivering results, and avoid inessential work. Each chapter includes action items and resources, along with stories of other leaders you'll want to learn from.

You don't need to follow the order laid out in the table of contents. Each skill stands on its own, so you can create your own sequence. Just immerse yourself in one or two that seem relevant. Work hard on them; you will use them throughout your work life.

At the end of every week you should sit down to review your progress in developing your skill and outline your follow-up steps. Unless you have an impeccable memory for details, you should be armed with notes you've taken during the week. These don't have to be lengthy—in fact, they shouldn't be, just a few words that capture the essence of the activity, conversation, or thought. I make my brief notes either on a small ruled pad I carry in my pocket or on my smart phone. It might take less than fifteen minutes; it might take half an hour. Keep the learning simple and move on, but make it a routine. Larry Bossidy, the successful former CEO of Honeywell, took an hour every Sunday to reflect on the people who reported to him, how they were doing, what they might need, and how they might be deployed better. He became a fantastic judge of people. For example, it was he who recommended Dave Cote as his successor; it was a very good pick.

Part II will help you identify when and how to make exponential leaps in your capability and capacity, what you can expect to learn, and how to recover from a bad move. Not every leap requires a job change, but some will. You will likely have to take risks to test your ability to learn and grow, and there may be times when you have to leave your company. As you progress, you will face hurdles, many of them social—annoyance, misunderstandings, and even jealousy. Your psychological as well as your cognitive strength will be tested.

Realizing your potential requires some degree of personal sacrifice. At every leap, you should weigh your ambition in the business world against what you want in the rest of your life. It is a balance that is different for everyone and might very well change over time. At some point, you may feel compelled to redefine success.

How Leadership Developers Should Use This Book

Senior leaders, HR departments, learning experts, and bosses can skip to Part III of this book, which will help you fill your pipeline with leadership talent that is relevant to the current business environment. You will have to face the dangerous reality that today's hipos will leave unless they can progress into the kinds of jobs they are capable of handling. That will require breaking conventions about job promotions and at times shaking up existing jobs to make room for the most promising hipos.

HR professionals will have to be assertive in working with management to transform the processes for identifying, developing, and retaining leaders. You should be prepared to challenge their basic assumptions and usual practices in favor of a new set of principles, like the ones mapped out in Chapter 9. It used to be that bosses controlled the fate of the people who reported to them; now, however, leadership talent should be seen as a resource to be managed and grown for the benefit of the organization as a whole. And development plans should be customized for each individual, using this book as a tool. The payback in terms of muscle building the organization will justify the time you spend on customizing careers for your hipos.

This is a time for creativity when it comes to providing chances for hipos to make leaps. It could be inclusion on a project team, or having the person go with more senior people on client calls, as one large advertising firm has begun to do. McKinsey's managing director, Dom Barton, has young recruits, two at a time, shadow him for a year. The young people have real responsibilities, but the exposure to clients around the world expands their view of the work that lies ahead. Hipos at a big industrial Indian company are given background information and asked to do their own research on the industry and macro environment. They then meet with senior people, who explain the company strategy and solicit reactions from the younger people. It's not just a matter of yes-ing the bosses; the senior people are expected to pay attention to what the younger people say.

Leadership developers may have to step in to resolve problems when millennials break the unwritten rules and leapfrog others. Older people may not like reporting to someone who is relatively young and untested. It will take thoughtful care to maintain the overall health of the social system while developing and rewarding hipos in ways that get them ready and make them want to stay. Supporting hipos in building their people skills and emotional intelligence will also help smooth the way.

A Final Word

The newest generation of leaders feel strongly about wanting to make the world a better place. But who doesn't?

Economic growth, on the whole, improves the lives of people everywhere, and business leaders are the front-line drivers of growth. The better the leader, the more value is being added to the world, and the higher the standard of living. So we all have a stake in seeing high-potential leaders build the capabilities they need to succeed.

Practiced well, leadership is indeed a higher calling and a chance to make the world a better place.

Hipo Self-Test and Development Guide – Chapter 1

You should decide for yourself whether you are a "hipo," regardless of whether your company has put you on their watch list. The following self-test can help you assess where you stand and also give you insights on where to focus as you develop your potential further.

Are You a High-Potential Leader?

Do the following descriptors apply to you? Is this what others would say about you? Consider delivering superior results that are sustainable a prerequisite, then rate yourself on each statement using the following scale:

1 = Not at all like me	4 = Frequently like me
2 = Occasionally like me	5 = Always like me
3 = Like me	

Question Number	Question	Your Rating
1	I have crystal-clear goals for what I want to achieve.	
2	I enjoy coaching and developing people.	
3	I have big ideas for how to improve my organization.	
4	I regularly take time to review our customers' end-to-end experience.	
5	I have an insatiable drive to learn.	
6	I keep up with the latest technology.	
7	I have a change-the-world mentality.	
8	I'm comfortable and effective in delegating tasks.	
9	I tend to look at people's strengths and find ways to build on them.	
10	I have an effective process for assessing and testing my new ideas.	
11	I'm well informed on our top competitors and stay up-to-date on their strategy, leaders, and customer perceptions.	
12	I enjoy connecting with people and have a wide-ranging network.	
13	I take in a lot of information from many sources.	
14	I imagine on a large scale.	
15	I ensure that my team's work processes are efficient and effective.	

(continued)

(continued)

Question Number	Question	Your Rating
16	When someone on my team isn't delivering results, I address the problem quickly.	
17	I create effective timelines for staging and managing my projects.	
18	I'm familiar with our company's providers and partners and the technology platforms that connect us.	
19	I have a regular reading practice that keeps me well informed.	
20	I can quickly process complex situations.	
21	I seek out whatever I need to make things happen.	
22	I have systems in place to effectively monitor and manage new information.	
23	In conversations, I tend to focus on positive solutions and common goals.	
24	I'm known as someone who asks thoughtful and incisive questions.	
25	I regularly scan news and media looking for emerging trends and game-changing people and events.	
26	I frequently have conversations with people from diverse backgrounds.	
27	I adapt quickly to new situations.	
28	I think in terms of the "big picture."	
29	I regularly review the people and projects I manage to ensure that the right people are in the right jobs.	
30	I communicate and collaborate across business units or functions to help achieve organizational goals.	
31	I'm known as a leader who can deliver results.	
32	I'm aware of how technological advances are impacting my industry and changing the competitive landscape.	
33	I enjoy attending learning events such as seminars, conferences, or classes.	
34	I have diverse social networks.	
35	I enjoy multiplying the energy and skills of those around me.	

Hipo Scoring Guide

To assess where you stand relative to other high-potential leaders, look up your responses (in the questionnaire above) to the specific question numbers listed below. Write your rating in the chart next to the question number. Then add up all the ratings to find your total score.

Your Scores			Sample			Interpreting Your Score	
Question Number	Your Rating		Question Number	Your Rating		Your Total Score	Likelihood That You Are a Hipo
6			6	4		41–50	Very High
7			7	5		31–40	High
13			13	3		26–30	Moderate
14			14	5		10–25	Low
21			21	4			
25			25	4			
27			27	4			
28			28	5			
34			34	3			
35			35	5			
TOTAL			TOTAL	42			

Development Scoring Guide

The scoring guides below will give you insights on where to focus your time and attention to get the most out of your potential. Repeat the same score transfer process you used before for each of the question numbers listed in the charts below.

Your Scores

Question Number	Your Score	Question Number	Your Score	Question Number	Your Score	Question Number	Your Score	Question Number	Your Score
1		2		3		4		5	
8		9		10		11		12	
15		16		17		18		19	
22		23		24		25		26	
29		30		31		32		33	
Skill #1 TOTAL		Skill #2 TOTAL		Skill #3 TOTAL		Skill #4 TOTAL		Skill #5 TOTAL	

Chapter 2	Chapter 3	Chapter 4	Chapter 5	Chapter 6
Increase the Return on Your Time (ROYT)	Multiply the Energy and Skills of Those Around You	Be a Master of Big Ideas and Execution	Get to Know Customers, Competitors, and the Macro Environment	Build Your Mental Capacity

(continued)

(*continued*)

Sample

Question Number	Your Score	Question Number	Your Score	Question Number	Your Score	Question Number	Your Score	Question Number	Your Score
1	3	2	5	3	3	4	3	5	5
8	4	9	5	10	1	11	4	12	5
15	3	16	4	17	3	18	3	19	2
22	4	23	5	24	4	25	3	26	5
29	2	30	4	31	3	32	4	33	4
Skill #1 TOTAL	16	Skill #2 TOTAL	23	Skill #3 TOTAL	14	Skill #4 TOTAL	17	Skill #5 TOTAL	21

Chapter 2	Chapter 3	Chapter 4	Chapter 5	Chapter 6
Increase the Return on Your Time (ROYT)	Multiply the Energy and Skills of Those Around You	Be a Master of Big Ideas and Execution	Get to Know Customers, Competitors, and the Macro Environment	Build Your Mental Capacity

Interpreting Results

In the sample above, this leader is very strong in skills #2 and #5. His weakest skill is #3, so he might want to put more of his development time into the skills related to "Be a Master of Big Ideas and Execution." However, the leader is also not as strong in Skill #1: "Increase the Return on Your Time." Since this ROYT skill helps free up more time in your day, he could also start there and then use the extra time he creates to focus on increasing his strategy and execution skills.

Notice what skills you scored highest and lowest in. Do these results make sense to you? Does the pattern suggest which skill would be the best place to start? It's up to you. Remember, you don't need to read this book front to back. Start with the skill that will give you the most impact now.

Tips for Hipos—How to Use This Book

First, decide for yourself whether you are a hipo. It doesn't matter whether you scored low on the self-test, or if your company doesn't have you on their watch list. If you *decide* that you're a hipo, you can use the ideas in this book to increase your potential and "up your game" as a leader.

You will advance faster if you create your own development path.

- Getting Started

  - Review your development scores on page 17 and then skim the checklists at the end of Chapters 2 through 6 to decide which skill is most important for you to expand first.

  - Read the chapter for that skill thoroughly. Print the Coaching Checklist at the end of the chapter, or scan it to store on your phone.

  - You'll reach your leadership potential through the disciplined routine practice of essential skills combined with periodic leaps.

  - The checklist supports your disciplined practice. It's what I would focus on if I were coaching you in person.

  - Keep the checklist where you'll see it every day, and build simple daily actions into your schedule to start developing the capabilities.

- Building Momentum

  - Take quick notes throughout the week and store them in a single notebook, file, or app.

  - At the end of every week, sit down to review your progress. A short session is fine, but make it a consistent weekly discipline.

  - Ask yourself these three questions:
    1. What new ideas have I experimented with?
    2. What have I learned?
    3. What follow-up steps will I take?

  - Developing skills through daily, weekly, monthly practice may seem uninspiring, but it's absolutely essential for reaching your goals.

- Planning Your Leap

  - Chapter 7 helps you identify when and how to make the big leaps that can exponentially increase your capability and capacity.

  - Plan to make your next leap after you are successful in your current role—when it has stopped stretching you or bringing any new learning opportunities.

  - Meanwhile, focus on building the hipo skills you need to be successful where you are right now.

  - You can also work on building the skills you'll need for the next step along your runway.

  - At every leap, weigh your ambition in the business world against what you want in the rest of your life. That balance is different for everyone, and might change over time.

Tips for HR and Leadership Developers—How to Use This Book

- Senior leaders, HR professionals, learning experts, and bosses can skip to Chapter 9. You'll find insights there on how the best companies I've worked with find, develop, manage, and monitor their hipos.

- If part of your role involves coaching others:

  - The checklists at the end of Chapters 2 through 6 will give you additional development ideas for them.

  - Chapter 7 can help you plan their next leaps and help them avoid the pitfalls that have derailed other hipos during their rapid advancement.

- And last but not least, don't forget about your own well-being.

    - The checklist at the end of Chapter 8 will give you ideas on how to create a more balanced and fulfilling life for yourself, as well as for guiding the people on your team.

    - Your role in developing the next generation of leaders who will drive our world economy is essential. Thank you for letting me be a part of your own learning journey as you fulfill this important task.

PART I

FIVE ESSENTIAL SKILLS FOR HIGH-POTENTIAL LEADERS

2

Increase the Return on Your Time (ROYT)

If you're like most hipos I know, your biggest complaint is that you don't have enough time to do everything you need to do, especially as you rise in an organization and face larger and more complex projects and challenges. There's a limit to how much you can expand your working hours without ruining your health or damaging your personal relationships. (Sleeping less is not the best option.) But just as you can raise the return on your money by smart investing, you can learn techniques to raise the return on your time. Leveraging your multipliers—those things that allow you to accomplish more—will free your time and mental space to focus on bigger things, including your own learning and self-improvement, while delivering excellent results.

Get Comfortable with People Better Than You

At one point in my career, I decided to call some of my former students from when I was teaching at Harvard Business School. Several had become CEOs of very large companies when they were only in their forties, and I wanted to hear about their experiences. I remembered that I had given one of them a rather poor grade, but when I called him he was profusely polite. "Please come see me.

You can stay at the house," he offered. "And let me know anything that you need."

I accepted the invitation. After a pleasant dinner, his wife dismissed herself, and he and I talked over glasses of wine. I apologized about giving him a low grade, but he said not to worry, he had learned a lot from the class. Then I posed some questions that had been on my mind: How was he able to move up so quickly? And what might up-and-coming leaders learn from his success? He was momentarily pensive, then replied:

"When I left school it became clear to me that the most important resource I had was time. I decided that I had to somehow create more time within the day. I thought about what would free me up the most, and I came up with three things. First, I had to become really good at hiring the right people and putting them in the right jobs. Second, if I saw that somebody wasn't up to the job, I had to move them out quickly. When I paid more attention to those things, I saw a difference in how much time I had. Third, I started planning six months ahead of time what I would no longer do—the things I would pass on to others. I decided who would take them over and what would have to happen to get that person ready."

My former student understood that your highest leverage is not process, organization, or money. It's people. Every task from creating a strategy to implementing a marketing plan depends on the quality of the people responsible for it. Yet leaders consistently fall short when it comes to hiring, developing, and promoting the best people for the work at hand, for a variety of reasons. They get preoccupied with matters that seem more pressing at the time. Or they pick people they're comfortable with without considering others who may be better suited to the job. Or they settle for the "best person available" without expanding or extending the search.

It takes a deep personal commitment to devote the time and energy to ensure that you have the very best person in each of the jobs you oversee. You may want help from HR or recruiting firms, but this is your personal responsibility. The better you are at it, the more you expand your own capacity and capability.

Dig in to fully understand the requirements of the job and how it may change over time, and be systematic and objective in assessing people. Take a simple example of the job of a sales rep. Maybe it used to require terrific interpersonal skills and product knowledge, but if the company is moving toward selling solutions, not just products, the same job will require broader business skills and more strategic thinking than before.

For any leadership position you fill, look for people who can do the job as you have defined it, but also look to the future. How does that job need to evolve, and can the person grow with it? Does the person have a history of innovative or entrepreneurial thinking? That can indicate the ability not only to grow with a job but also to adapt to changing markets. Suppose your company needs to escape from a maturing business by expanding beyond manufacturing and into services. If all of your leaders are coming out of manufacturing, their experience might be limiting.

If you're uncomfortable hiring people outside your band of loyal followers, try to pinpoint your psychological blockage. Maybe you're afraid to take a risk on people. If that's the case, push yourself. Do your best to calibrate the person and take a chance; then later reflect on where you went right or wrong. That's how your judgment will improve.

Maybe you are settling too soon because you didn't find someone who matched your criteria. Be tenacious and keep searching. I know one CEO who withstood heavy pressure from the board and others when the position as head of R&D went unfilled for two years. It was crucially important to get the right person for the job, and it took that long for the CEO to find him.

Another common blockage is being afraid to hire people better than you, yet hipos succeed because they do precisely that. It may seem like a good idea when you are a CEO, but as a junior level leader, it can be very threatening. Spencer Rascoff, CEO of online real estate marketplace Zillow, shared his view with *New York Times* interviewer Adam Bryant: "The biggest mistake I tend to see from junior managers is not hiring people who are better than them. It might be subconscious—people don't want to be shown up by one of their direct reports—or maybe they don't know how to identify talent." [i]

Lacking the confidence to recruit strong, capable people or to give them big responsibilities where their talents can shine—and perhaps outshine yours—is especially risky in today's world, where companies need an infusion of new skills on a regular basis. Reluctance to hire people with technical capabilities you lack will compromise the company's performance and your own. Watch for this in your own behavior and go the other way. Recruit stars for your team, people with skills beyond your own, and your own capacity and ability to deliver results will expand.

Set and Reset Your Priorities

Most hipos want to be comprehensive—to do everything that's important, and do it well—but their time and concentration soon get diluted. You will be far more effective if you narrow your priorities to the few that will have the greatest impact on your business. Determining these is the result of having clear goals, knowing the realities of your business, and making a judgment about what matters most. It is a mental activity that you hone with practice.

Make a clear distinction between goals and priorities. For me, a goal is a crystal-clear description of what you want to achieve. Sometimes you'll set the goals yourself, sometimes they'll be set for you. Either way you need total clarity about what needs to be achieved.

The best goals, meaning those that produce a healthy outcome for the business, have several components, all of which can be

---

[i] Adam Bryant, "Don't Be Scared to Hire Someone Better Than You," *New York Times*, December 19, 2013.

achieved at the same time. A narrow singular goal such as boosting sales or reducing costs by a certain percentage, can do a lot of damage by encouraging people to cut corners or sacrifice the long term for the sake of meeting the target.

Priorities are basically the actions you take to achieve your goals. You have to decide which ones matter most. Use your knowledge of external and internal realities to decide. Let's say you head a General Motors division and you are striving to increase market share by one point, cut costs by 3 percent, and increase cash flow by 5 percent over the next three years. The probability of achieving those goals will be heavily affected by whether your Japanese competitors have a price advantage because of changes in the value of the yen. If you believe the yen will depreciate heavily and that the decline will be sustained, giving the Japanese an edge, you may want to change your product mix to minimize damage from price wars on products with thin margins. Changing the product mix would then be a dominant priority.

Think about priorities in a time frame: What do you have to accomplish this quarter, this year, and three years out? To be sure you're not sacrificing your medium- and long-term goals, translate them into specific actions that will be taken now. That is, what do you have to do in the short term to build the long term?

Setting priorities is an iterative process. Think about what you need to do, and group the tasks so they can be assigned to the individuals who can make them happen. Keep culling the list until it is a small number of tasks that will have a big impact on your ability to achieve the goals. Ultimately, you will want a set of three to five what I call laser-sharp dominant priorities. Arriving at these, keeping intense focus on them, and driving them relentlessly is key to execution.

What about your boss's priorities? To some extent, other people's priorities will be a fact of life for you, even if you're a manager reporting to a VP or a CEO reporting to the board. But it's still up to you to ensure that you are focusing your time on what you think is most important. Some urgent things need to be dealt with and may change your agenda, but if that's the norm rather than the exception every time you open your e-mail, you will become far less effective than your hipo counterparts. You have to learn how to say no to some things that are demanding your attention (or at least to fend them off for the moment) in order to accomplish the most important priorities on your own list.

It's not unusual for your view of what's important to differ from your boss's. Yours may be better informed, if, for example, you do a better job of scanning the externals, have a broader bandwidth, or have better access to internal information. Any of that could be the result of programs you've attended, assignments you've been given, or networks you've developed precisely because you are a hipo. You might be more attuned to communications the CEO or analyst community sends out. If you work for a hipo leader, it may be a different story, but many bosses are narrowly focused on delivering their quarterly numbers. They don't have the breadth of a hipo. How you handle this interpersonally is crucial. You can't be smug. You have to be sensitive to the priorities the boss is giving you, because she, too, has to deliver something to her boss. You have to support that to remain in her good graces. Use your business savvy and interpersonal skills to try to exert influence, but don't destroy the relationship.

It's important to clear your plate at routine intervals—that is, to periodically look for tasks and projects that have become less relevant and can be dropped, as my former student did. Of those that remain, ask yourself what only you must do now and what might be passed to someone else. Then make a plan for who will take on those other things—and when. It will likely take time to prepare someone else, or perhaps to recruit someone. If you follow the rule of hiring people better than yourself, they will likely be anxious to learn and grow by taking on new challenges and responsibilities.

Customize Your Information Flow

Available information grows exponentially year after year with no end in sight. That's a good thing to the extent that it adds to the stock of human knowledge, but so-called "information fatigue syndrome" is widely blamed for decreased productivity, higher stress, and chronic irritability. Clearly there's more than you can possibly pay attention to—including reams of advice on how to manage the deluge.

The Internet is an increasingly useful filter for information as more and more sites and search engines enable you to customize alerts, briefings, and condensed news items. They can help ensure that you are aware of all the top stories related to your company, competitors, marketplace, and industry while saving you hours of reading time. To take just one example, the *Financial Times*'s ft.com/alertshub currently offers registered subscribers a wealth of choices such as business news summaries and updates, market briefings, and company updates, all sorted by region. Premium subscribers can choose to receive alerts on up to thirty specific companies. Google offers free news alerts that you can customize to any specific search criteria you choose. If hard copy is your preference, both *The Wall Street Journal* and *Financial Times* each offer well-chosen news roundups in extremely concise form. In *The Wall Street Journal*, the "What's News" column on the left side of the front page is a time-saver.

I review my alerts during my reading time each day and bookmark or clip articles I want to explore later. Whether you store them on your tablet or in a manila file folder, keep them with you for quick access. By "quick access" I mean always at hand to fill unexpected blank spaces in your schedule. I've had some of my most productive reading time while waiting for a delayed flight or sitting in a taxi in rush-hour traffic.

You no doubt need a lot of data to do your job, but there is an overabundance of it today in virtually every organization—more than an individual can possibly review. At many companies, the use of dashboards is routine. Even a P&L statement on Excel can be thought of as a dashboard, because it provides a quick and easy way to track performance. You might want to create your own version of a dashboard. Given that your skill as a leader lies in being able to extract insights from data, shaping the kinds of information you receive and how it is presented will be tremendously beneficial. Take charge of it. Zillions of things are measured, but keep it simple. Decide what is important to know, and how frequently that information should come to you. The data you most need might not be captured by the company-wide dashboards, but if it exists on a server somewhere, the IT department might be willing to capture it for you. Then ask for help formatting that information so you can easily spot patterns and aberrations, whether it's through the use of graphic displays, pictures, or numbers.

You probably generate far more internal reports than any individual could possibly read. Take a look at the standard reports that your team creates—and that you have to review. Decide on the optimal schedule for seeing that data. If you only have time to look at that weekly report a couple of times a month, can you change the schedule so it's generated only twice a month? Or could some of the legacy reports that no one looks at anymore be eliminated altogether? This frees up your time, and that of everyone involved in creating the reports.

Not every report in the company is compulsory reading. For every new one you ask for or automatically receive, give an expiration date. For example, say, "Could you send me this report on the first day of the month for the next quarter? If we discover that we can't live without it, I'll be back in touch to ask you to continue it. If you don't hear from me, you can stop sending it."

E-mail is the AK-47 of communications, and it can mow you down if you don't take defensive measures. That flow of information must also be managed. A few simple guidelines can help clear the clutter: Don't open your e-mail until you've devoted the first hour of your day solely to your top priority; create e-mail–free time zones during your day so you can focus on important projects without interruption; and use automatic sorting to group e-mail by category or project to make reading and responding faster.

Delegate and Follow Through

You should be spending your time on things only you need to do and delegating the rest. That is often easier said than done for a hipo. Delegating may be difficult because you think no one else can do things as well as you can, but your performance will suffer if you can't relinquish control and hand projects off to others. Alex Gorsky, CEO of Johnson & Johnson, says that was a challenge for him, but he learned early that "it's not really what I do. It's about bringing together a group of people who have different skills, different capabilities, and working through them to accomplish a particular task."[ii]

How you meet your own commitments is important. Are you doing it by draining energy—driving people relentlessly, or burning them out by making impossible demands? Or are you expanding the capacity of the organization by helping people grow and expand their own capacities? In other words, there's a right and a wrong way to delegate.

Learn to delegate well. What *doesn't* work is assigning a task without knowing that the person is capable of delivering on it, remaining uninvolved until the end of the time period, then blaming others when results don't materialize. As a general rule, you should delegate tasks to the lowest possible organizational level, and to a particular person, and you must be sure the person has the necessary expertise and information to complete the job. Allocate time to help the person along by providing any necessary training or coaching, and make yourself accessible to answer questions as they arise.

[ii] Knowledge@Wharton, "Leadership Challenges at Johnson & Johnson," January 9, 2014.

Remember that the additional responsibility you assign will likely be an opportunity for the person to grow, and your own capacity will expand as his or hers does, so it's important to help the person succeed. If there's no one in your immediate group who is up to the task, maybe you can attract a hipo from another function or business unit who could take it on as a way to broaden his or her experience.

Give the entire task to one individual, not a team. It's faster and more efficient: the person won't need to achieve consensus to make decisions and will own the task completely. Communicate clearly what you're asking for, being sure to break down concepts into specific action items. Identify the goals, controls, and boundaries, and furnish a context, explaining why it needs to be done, its importance in the overall scheme of things, and the possible complications that may arise. Articulate the end results you expect and the standards you'll use to measure successful completion. If the task requires collaboration with others, make sure to communicate with them, too, so they understand that you expect them to participate.

Focus on the "what," not the "how." Detailing how the work should be done is micromanaging, and it's destructive all around; if you interfere without good reason you'll lose the person's enthusiasm and commitment. Allow the person to devise her own methods and processes. If she is clear and committed, then trust her.

Trust But Verify

Many leaders feel their work is done once they've assigned the person and clearly laid out the expectations, but that's hardly the case. Now comes a true test of your ability to execute: the discipline of follow-through. As people start down the path, they're likely to run into roadblocks of one kind or another. They may start out gung-ho, then unarticulated doubts or questions creep in. They lose momentum. Maybe the person runs into a colleague who won't provide the information he's asked for. Repeatedly. Or the person can't persuade the engineering department to lend their expertise on a product development project, or is running through the allocated funds much faster than expected because of macro-economic factors. Maybe they misunderstood what was being asked of them.

It's your job to discover the problems and make sure they are resolved promptly. You'll unearth them sooner if you review progress at agreed-upon intervals. These check-ins, say once a week, in person or by phone, should have real substance to them. Skip the superficial questions about how things are going, and don't accept perfunctory answers that everything is just fine. You have to ask probing questions such as, What is going better than expected? and What's the biggest risk to completing the project on time? The point is to understand any real-world problems that are arising without rushing to blame. Frequent check-ins are also a chance to acknowledge good work, which is energizing.

Delegating and following through are critical to excellence in execution. To be sure, some people have risen far in their companies without this skill. They build their personal brand as a high-level thinker. They love the intellectual excitement of new concepts and thrive in the world of grasping and explaining strategies. Details bore them. They're willing to delegate, but they don't know how to convert their ideas into specific tasks and they don't follow through. These leaders put themselves and their companies at risk. The best leaders think big and conceptualize, while never losing sight of the discipline behind execution, and in fact, their strategic thinking is grounded in reality because of it. (For more on execution, see Chapter 4.)

Decide How to Leverage Yourself

You may be highly skilled as a salesperson or technical expert, but you have to redefine how you will add value as you become responsible for overseeing other people's work. At some point people should no longer be coming to you for your technical advice. They should see you as helping them develop and use their own. Be clear in your mind about how you will and will not add value, and when and how you will help others achieve the common goal.

Pat Gallagher is the third generation to lead the Chicago-based risk management insurance brokerage his grandfather founded, and he has grown the business to be the fourth largest insurance brokerage in the United States with a market capitalization of more than $8 billion. He describes a crucial transition he made when his father and uncle chose him from among his age-mates as their protégé. He had worked as a file boy since the age of fourteen, then as an intern, and then became a sales rep after college, a job that came naturally to him. "I got my license and started cold-calling, asking people if they'd let us work on their insurance. I loved it from the beginning, and I was pretty good at it. I was one of the biggest producers in the company, he says."

A few years later, Gallagher's father and uncle put him in charge of a sales unit. "Then it was a matter of leveraging expertise," Gallagher recalls. "Instead of me going out and selling one account, I could influence five or six at a time."

He recounts a story typical of how he made it work: "We had an account that was a mechanical contractor that assembled and transported big, heavy factory equipment. It had been my account, and the other person who was on it couldn't break through to make the sale. I thought it might help if someone with the Gallagher name joined in, so the two of us paid a visit. We gave a great proposal, but the client still was nervous as a cat, maybe because we both were young. That's when I decided to get my dad involved. He met with the client saying, 'Look, I wouldn't put my company's reputation on the line if I didn't know my son and his producer were really good.' The client's face lit up, and things went well after that.

"The value I brought to that proposition was two-fold: I went with the sales guy as a confident manager knowing that we had done the best job on the proposal, and I read the situation well enough to come back and ask my dad to make the call. The outcome was positive for all of us."

Your contribution may come in the form of mustering resources—human or otherwise—as it was for Gallagher, or opening lines of communication, or resolving a conflict. Focusing precisely on how you can help others do their jobs should be a big part of doing yours.

Create Repeatable Processes

You inherit a lot of systems and processes when you come into a job, some of which have outlasted their usefulness. As a hipo, you likely have little patience for reports, meetings, and decision-making processes that are slow and bureaucratic. You can double or triple your capacity by finding those that can be eliminated, automated, or streamlined, freeing up people's time for more meaningful work. If you are delegating well, you might be able to cut layers out of the approval process, for example.

You can't eliminate systems completely. Think about what kinds of communication, information flows, and decision-making processes are essential, and make them routine, keeping in mind that organizations of every size, including yours, need consistent processes to grow. Maybe you need information from the frontline sales people three levels below you to make good marketing decisions, but you're frustrated by how slowly that information is fed up through the hierarchical layers. Create a mechanism to get the input directly, maybe through a combination of real-time data and weekly conference calls with store managers.

In the early 1990s, Walmart founder Sam Walton created a process whereby senior management had weekly conference calls with a sample of thirty regional managers who were charged with visiting competitors' stores the week before. During the call, the managers weighed in on what the competition was doing in terms of product offerings, merchandise displays, and price. They also compared notes on what was or was not selling well in their stores. This routine meeting created a direct flow of information to the top-most decision makers and allowed the company to respond quickly to shifts in the market.

Since then, digital platforms and algorithms have been transforming retail and virtually every other industry. You should be thinking about what data analytics can generate and how to combine it with the kinds of insights, expertise, and judgments only people can provide. For example, you might want to eliminate a dull weekly staff meeting in favor of a brief check-in during which a group reflects on how to respond given what the data analytics are telling them.

Any such mechanism you create should be scalable, meaning it can continue to function as your organization grows. And some may be applicable to your next job.

Be Decisive

Efforts to improve the return on your time will not amount to much if you have trouble making decisions. An analytic mind is an asset, but if you are perpetually seeking more information, more facts, more alternatives, and more certainty, you will waste time going down rabbit holes. Meanwhile, the train will leave the station without you.

The issue of analysis paralysis is hitting many business leaders who are temperamentally uncomfortable with ambiguity. You have to accept the fact that some information will be fuzzy and that some variables might go in a different direction than what you assumed—and make a decision anyway. Put simply, uncertainty is a fact of life.

On the other hand, seat-of-the-pants decision making is no better, especially without a deep experience base. Sometimes a seasoned business leader appears to be shooting from the hip when in fact the person has quickly discerned patterns and key facts based on decades of experience. That is something that is earned through years of systematic thinking and testing of one's judgment.

You have to know the difference between weighing the relevant facts and losing time because you're dodging the issue. Maybe you are a linear thinker, or a numbers jock. You like the certainty of knowing what the result will be: two plus two equals four. If you allow that tendency to slow your decision making or lead you to making only fail-safe, incremental decisions, you will not be a hipo for long. You will have to overcome your natural tendencies in order to move into bigger jobs. Former U.S. General Colin Powell's 40-70 rule is a good guideline. He believes that if you have less than 40 percent of the information, you shouldn't make a decision. But if you wait until you have more than 70 percent of the information, you've waited too long. He says, "Once the information is in the 40 to 70 range, go with your gut."

The more aware you are of what blocks your decisiveness—whether it's arrogance, fear of adverse repercussions, an aversion to risk, or previous failures—the more likely you are to expand your potential. Like many people, you may have difficulty overcoming the blockages by yourself. You can get help by finding people in your working group who can point it out to you, someone who observes you and can give you specific feedback. It could be your boss or mentor, but could also be a peer, a friend, or someone outside the company. Take some well-calculated risks when you are in the 40-70 zone, and learn from your successes and failures. Like any skill, decision making is improved with practice, and decision making in the face of uncertainty is an essential hipo skill.

Hipo Coaching Checklist – Chapter 2
Increase the Return on Your Time (ROYT)

☐ 1. Clarify Your Goals
- Be crystal clear about what you are trying to achieve. If your goals have several components, do they all have some internal consistency; that is, can they be achieved at the same time?
- Write down each goal, clearly and concisely.

(continued)

(*continued*)

- If your manager sets your goals, take the time to clarify them yourself.
- What are the key components?
- What will the end-state look like when the goal is achieved?
- Who are the stakeholders—and how can you get them on board?
- What resources will you need, and how can you get them?
- How does the goal tie into the larger framework of the organization as a whole?
- If you discover that elements of your goals are contradictory, check back with your boss to clarify.

☐ **2. Set and Reset Your Priorities**
- Identify your priorities—the actions you will take to achieve the goals.
- You can have several priorities, but since time and budgets are limited, you need to decide which ones matter most. Ask yourself, which actions will give you the greatest impact?
- Keep culling the list until you have a set of three to five laser-sharp dominant priorities—each with its own set of sub-tasks that can be delegated to others.
- Map out your priorities in a time frame: What do you have to accomplish this month, this quarter, this year, and three years out?
- Translate longer-term goals into specific actions that will be taken now. Working backward can sometimes help. If you need to deliver the results in two years, what needs to be in place at eighteen months? At twelve months? At six months? Now?
- Review your priorities monthly and adjust for any changes that have happened in your company or the marketplace.

☐ **3. Ensure You Have the Right People in the Right Jobs**
- Review the people and projects you manage quarterly from a staffing perspective.
- Do the job positions still match what you need to accomplish?
- What skills does each position need?
- Does the person in that position have those skills? If not, can she or he learn the skills? What resources are needed to support the learning?
- Is the person engaged and motivated? If not, see Chapter 3 for ways to address poor performance.

☐ **4. Continually Evolve Your To-Do List**
- Plan six months ahead of time what parts of your job you will no longer do.

- Decide who can take on your old tasks, and what you need to do to get them ready.
- What things have you already mastered that you can delegate?
- Who can you develop to manage the processes you have redesigned, or oversee projects that are on track and no longer challenge you?
- The more time you can free up from the mundane, the more you'll have available for the next big project or new role. Consider what you'd like to add to your to-do list.

☐ **5. Delegate and Follow Through**
  - As a general rule, delegate tasks to the lowest possible organizational level, and to a single person who has the necessary expertise and information to complete the job.
  - Communicate clearly what you're asking for.
  - Break down concepts into specific action items.
  - Identify the goals, controls, and boundaries, and furnish a context, explaining why it needs to be done, its importance in the overall scheme of things, and the possible complications that may arise.
  - Articulate the end results you expect and the standards you'll use to measure successful completion.
  - If the task requires collaboration with others, make sure to communicate with them, too, so they understand that you expect them to participate.
  - Allocate time to help the person by providing any necessary training or coaching, and make yourself accessible to answer questions as they arise.
  - To avoid micromanaging, focus on the "what," not the "how." Allow the person to devise her own methods and processes.
  - Review progress at agreed-upon intervals, perhaps weekly for novices or monthly for those who are more experienced with the tasks.
  - Ask probing questions such as:
    - What is going better than expected?
    - What's the biggest risk to completing the project on time?
    - What surprises have you run into?
  - Frequent check-ins are also a chance to acknowledge good work, which is energy creating.

☐ **6. Take Charge of Information**
  - Set up automated news alerts or customized news sources to stay informed on topics related to your dominant priorities, key competitors, or emerging trends.
  - Assess these news sources quarterly to see whether they are adding real value. If not, replace them.

(continued)

(*continued*)

- Design a simple dashboard to manage internal data. Decide what you need to know, and how frequently that information should come to you. Then work with IT to create the reports you need.
- If reports outlive their usefulness, eliminate them.
- Don't open your e-mail until you've devoted the first hour of your day solely to your top priority.
- Create e-mail–free time zones during your day to focus on important projects without interruption.
- Use automatic sorting to group e-mail by category or projects to make reading and responding faster and to eliminate clutter.

☐ **7. Decide How to Leverage Yourself**
- Be clear about how you will and will not add value to other people's work.
- Don't cling to your role as the "go-to" person for expert advice.
- Use judgment in deciding when and how you will step in to help others achieve the common goal.

☐ **8. Create Repeatable Processes**
- Review your team's processes and any organizational processes that take up your team's time. Can any of these processes be eliminated, automated, or streamlined?
- Think about what data analytics can generate and how to combine it with the kinds of insights, expertise, and judgments only people can provide to get things done more efficiently.
- Be sure that any new processes or mechanisms you create are scalable, meaning they can continue to function as your organization grows.

☐ **9. Be Decisive**
- If you feel stuck, reflect on what blocks your decisiveness. Are you afraid of making a mistake? Waiting for more information or more certainty about the outcome? Avoiding personal risk? Or underconfident because of previous failures? Overcoming these blockages will expand your potential.
- To avoid "analysis paralysis," follow U.S. General Colin Powell's 40-70 rule. If you have less than 40 percent of the information, wait to make your decision. But if you wait until you have more than 70 percent of the information, you've waited too long. Powell says, "Once the information is in the 40 to 70 range, go with your gut."
- Decision making is improved with practice. Take some well-calculated risks when you are in the 40-70 zone, and learn from your successes and failures.

Additional Resources

Barker, Eric. "Achieving Goals: Everything You Need to Know." Blog post. Accessed November 21, 2016. http://www.bakadesuyo.com/2012/05/the-last-damn-thing-youll-ever-need-to-read-a/.

Charan, Ram. *Know-How: The 8 Skills That Separate People Who Perform from Those Who Don't*. New York: Crown Publishing Group, 2007.

Charan, Ram. *What the CEO Wants You to Know: How Your Company Really Works*. New York: Crown Publishing Group, 2001.

Drucker, Peter F. *The Effective Executive: The Definitive Guide to Getting the Right Things Done*. New York: HarperCollins Publishers, 2006.

Gawande, Atul. *The Checklist Manifesto: How to Get Things Right*. New York: Metropolitan Books, 2011.

Heath, Chip, and Dan Heath. *Decisive: How to Make Better Choices in Life and Work*. New York: Crown Publishing Group, 2013.

Keller, Gary, and Jay Papasan. *The ONE Thing: The Surprisingly Simple Truth Behind Extraordinary Results*. Austin, TX: Bard Press, 2013.

Useem, Michael. *The Leader's Checklist, Expanded Edition: 15 Mission-Critical Principles*. Philadelphia, PA: Wharton Digital Press, 2011.

3

Multiply the Energy and Skills of Those Around You

If you read Chapter 2, you know that hiring great people and putting them in the right jobs can increase your own capacity. Now I want to expand that point: the quality of the people you hire, how well they fit their jobs, and how well they work together determines much of your success and that of your organization. Think of it as a formula when you build your teams: People Quality + Job Fit + Collaboration = Team Performance.

People create strategy. People deliver the numbers. That means if you fall short on the people side, you fall short on business leadership, period. You have to invest considerable time to know and grow people and to *integrate* their work. You also have to face up to tough decisions about people, including removing those who drain energy from others. Some leaders make judgment calls on people and never look back. As a hipo, you can't afford to do that. Just because you've been allowed to hire and fire doesn't mean you're good at it. Work to develop your skills and judgment on the people side. Frankly, some companies undervalue this, but a growing number are making "develops other leaders" a requirement for advancement.

Identify a Person's God-Given Talent

The best way to power up your organization and your leadership is to improve your skill in judging and developing other people's talents. This applies to those you work with currently, even if they don't report to you, and anyone you are considering hiring. Think of yourself as a talent scout and coach, always watching for other people's natural strengths and imagining how to take them further. It's a skill I've seen many high-performing leaders practice with a passion. Last year when I was at the Microsoft Summit, I sat with a client who is the head of one of the world's largest and most successful global consumer companies. He built it from practically nothing over a period of about twenty years. I knew him to be patient and determined and to have terrific instincts about business. That day I saw another aspect of his leadership as he listened intently to the various leaders who spoke to the group. When one particular presenter had finished, my client leaned into me and said, "I like him. Introduce him to my son. We continue to look for superior managers." There was no doubt that this Brazilian company would make room for whatever talent its leaders spotted.

We know that every human being is different, that each has a unique blend of specific knowledge, personality traits, and cognitive abilities. We also know that performance in any number of jobs is affected by intangibles like attitude and optimism. That's what makes understanding people more challenging than understanding numbers. Even as new software applications are popping up regularly to support recruiting and performance evaluation, the human side—the part that can't be reduced to 1's and 0's and checklists— still matters. The better you are at analyzing talent, understanding it, shaping and building it, the more you will accomplish.

Your aim should be to see people in their entirety and accurately judge what they do really well—their "god's gift" if you will—so you can put them in jobs where they will flourish. This is not an idealistic notion. It's what great leaders do instinctively and many high-performing companies have institutionalized.

The value of pinpointing and nurturing a person's specific talent is obvious in the sports world, where coaches and scouts have a keen eye toward how an athlete's skills and personality will augment the team. They arm themselves with lots of data, but they also observe the person on and off the field. A basketball coach wants a great three-point shooter but also recognizes when a player is "a leader" who can energize the team and turn the game around. Those principles apply in business as well.

You probably have plenty of quantitative data to judge a person's performance, but don't leave it at that. What is he really good at? Skip the negatives for a moment, and think only about the positives. In two or three clear sentences, using simple everyday language, how would you describe this person? You should be able to capture something like this: "She has great command of facts and numbers. She sees patterns in the numbers. She will readily change her mind if the facts support a different view." Or "He builds strong relationships with customers. He knows how to position our offerings against the competition. He is a resource others turn to. He motivates the team."

You'll see a person's god's gift more accurately if you do two things: carefully observe the person's decisions and behaviors, and cross-check your observations with others. Watch, for example, how the person behaves in meetings. How does he handle disagreements? Does he listen to opposing views and try to find common ground or dig in his heels? Does he share information willingly? Does he come up with creative solutions? And does he elicit negative or positive behavior from others?

Most people are impressed or unimpressed in the first ten minutes they meet a person or hear her talk. They make conclusions based heavily on obvious personality traits, such as aggressiveness, confidence, and energy level. Go beyond those first impressions—consciously fight them if you formed them long ago—and drill to what is behind the person's comments and behavior. At one company I worked with, the CEO was questioning his intention to promote a leader after getting a lot of negative feedback about him. People said the person was too impatient and negative. The CEO took the complaints seriously, but as he probed the situation, he came to realize that the leader was merely frustrated after months of trying to gain support from his peers. Without their collaboration, he could not move forward on an initiative he knew to be of utmost importance to the company, and to the CEO. A better understanding of the context shed a different light on the executive's behavior.

Consider the quality of a person's decisions, but also the methodology she uses. Some people leap to conclusions, others become bogged down in analysis. Observe the points at which the person uses judgment versus strictly numerical facts. That will help you see the degree to which she is an intuitive thinker and how much risk she's willing to take. Her use of information, and especially its sources, will also give you insight into her personality and how her mind works. Does the person have diverse social networks and participate in groups that expose her to a range of perspectives? If you learned that a young leader had created an informal group of peers from different industries who meet on a regular basis to share what they see happening in the world, you should take it as a clear indication that she relishes new information and seeing the world from different vantage points.

You will have more insight into the person if you get to know her in a variety of settings. That's why some boards arrange dinners with up-and-coming leaders the night before the board meeting. At small tables conducive to informal conversation, directors are mixed with those who could someday succeed the CEO, so they have a chance to see the people beyond their polished PowerPoint presentations in the boardroom. Those occasions get the leaders off script and allow directors to drill more deeply into their thinking. I've known directors to completely change their view of someone's capability based on those conversations.

Don't trust your judgments about people without finding ways to verify them. We all have unconscious biases, and we're all at risk of forming opinions prematurely. You will hone your skill in identifying someone's god's gift by comparing what you see with other people's observations. One way to do this is by asking peers to identify the person's strengths. Use the same technique you apply to yourself: ask them to state in clear, simple sentences the positives about the person. Suggest that they be specific, "She is good at spotting unmet customer needs" versus "She is marketing-oriented," and ask for evidence. Any differences that emerge will give you something to watch for and explore further, but in almost all the cases I've seen, observations converge. The process turns impressionistic thinking into the truth of who the person is, so much so that the individual would likely say, "Yes, that's me!"

Think of how it applies to the late Steve Jobs of Apple, whose behaviors and actions are so well documented. I once asked a class at Wharton Business School to state his natural talent. Out came a lot of big words, like visionary, genius, game-changer, and entre-preneurial. As I pressed the group to be more specific, the scope narrowed into phrases like, "He figures out what will be a great product." "How?" I asked. And then the phrases got even sharper, "He understands what consumers will want, and he acts decisively." In the end, the description was specific, and it could be verified by looking at what he actually did. It would be hard to find anyone who would dispute that Jobs's natural talents were to imagine what consumers would want and would be willing to pay a premium price for; to search for discontinuities in the external landscape and figure out which direction to go to grab the opportunities in it; and to conceive and execute differentiated products and business models that would yield high margin and build the brand.

A modified version of this process will help you know more about people you hire from outside the company. HR departments tend to rely on résumés, key words, and testing to determine who is right for a job. You might find a stronger candidate by stepping outside the lines, being clear about the criteria that matter most, and de-emphasizing others that screen people out unnecessarily. You will find a better fit if you create a fuller picture of the candidates through reference checking beyond verifying dates and job titles. Spend more time talking with the person and with those who know her, asking for specific examples of how she makes decisions or gets results. Asking "how?" can open a vault of information about the person. After the interviews, don't forget to cross-check your impressions with someone else.

Build Other People's Strengths

Virtually every company has some kind of performance review process, but often it is merely a date on the calendar when a boss sits down to tell you what percentage salary increase you will get based on some broad measure of how you performed. Compensation affects motivation, but what really releases energy is the personal attention you give to helping people leverage and grow their talents. Rarely do performance reviews provide any of that. Those meetings are generally brief, uncomfortable, and yield little constructive feedback.

Having identified where a person's natural abilities lie, think of creative ways to build on those abilities. This should be an ongoing everyday activity for you. If you have a large number of people reporting to you, you won't have time to devote personal attention to everyone. Focus on those who are in the most influential jobs, but also keep a watchful eye for others who have high potential. Consider the jobs they have now and how they might be reshaped, or whether another job would allow the person to excel.

Expanding the talent of other hipos by finding jobs or tasks in which the person can make a leap is one of the greatest things you can do. If HR and senior leaders are watching for this as they ought to be, you will get a lot of credit. Even if they're not, you will experience firsthand the benefits of expanding your capacity by helping others expand theirs. I've known many leaders who were visited decades later by people who went on to big leadership jobs and came back to express their gratitude for having been given that initial chance to shine. There are risks involved. You don't want anyone to fail, but you have to accept the fact that stretch assignments are not risk-free.

Focusing on the positives doesn't mean you ignore shortcomings, or that there isn't room to improve. Another way to help multiply people's energy and skill is through constructive feedback. It's interesting to note that some leading-edge HR departments have disbanded the idea of annual performance reviews for any purpose other than adjusting compensation. Some are adopting technologies that support feedback in real time, where bosses, peers, and individuals can log comments that are collected online. The information is visible to the boss and the individual, who can immediately discuss any issues that arise. GE's system, based on a mobile app called PD@GE, also compiles the feedback messages into a summary at the end of the year. As of July 2016, it is being applied to its 200,000 salaried workers, replacing GE's existing performance review system. Early adopters like GE and Adobe are still working out the kinks, but their aim is to encourage frequent open dialogue about how well people are doing in their jobs and what they need to work on. That way people can adjust sooner, and there are no unpleasant surprises when they let pent-up frustrations go unexpressed too long.

Depending on where your company stands on this, you may need to create your own routine for providing direct, honest feedback, the more frequently the better. Choose one or two things the person should focus on, and be clear and specific. It could be a particular business skill the person needs to acquire, or it could be on the behavior side. A simple example is that of an accomplished leader who was being considered for a job reporting directly to the CEO. In that role, she would be making presentations to the board and at times interacting with major customers. One problem: she had a habit of using foul language, which was off-putting to her colleagues and clearly wouldn't fly in the boardroom. When it was brought to her attention, she worked to curb the habit, to the point where others got comfortable enough to move her up.

If you find direct, frequent interaction distasteful, keep working on it. The more you practice, the more comfortable you're likely to feel and the more pointed your feedback is likely to be. Don't give up on yourself too soon, but if you continue to hate that part of the job and can't remove the psychological barrier, you may have to consider a role as an individual contributor instead.

If, on the other hand, you master the art of giving the kind of constructive feedback that helps people grow, you will build a reputation as a great person to work for and you'll attract more hipos to your team. It happens at places like McKinsey, the esteemed consulting firm, where word gets out about partners who give younger people great opportunities to develop. These partners get their pick of cream-of-the-crop consultants for their project teams.

Don't forget to give people credit, especially for any extra effort they make. Public recognition, such as complimenting their work in front of their peers, goes a long way to make people feel appreciated. Within the guidelines your company gives you, reward the high performers disproportionately. Treating everyone the same breeds mediocrity and raises the risk that the best performers will leave. Don't take it personally if your hipos do decide to take a job elsewhere. By nature, they are seeking new opportunities. It's been said that when he was CEO of GE, Jack Welch took pride in seeing leaders take big jobs elsewhere, even those people he had personally invested in.

Make Necessary Changes Quickly

I have yet to meet a leader with a perfect record of judging people. When you make a mistake, you have to be intellectually honest with yourself and cut your losses. Give the person a chance, but don't drag your feet because you dread the conversation. Waiting too long to remove a non-performer has ended the careers of many senior leaders. In one case, a division head was underperforming because he wouldn't face up to the fact that one of the people reporting to him was completely mismatched to the job. His boss questioned why he kept the person in the job, and the division head admitted, "I hate this part of the job." With some coaching, the division head finally overcome his psychological blockage. He later told his boss, "My instincts were telling me I had to replace him. You gave me the courage to move."

Non-performers—the people who are repeatedly unable to do what they agreed to do—are anathema to high performance. If they don't improve, you have to move them as soon as possible. Many managers don't, because they want to be liked, they fear the person's reaction, or they've already invested so much in trying to make the person succeed. They underestimate the negative effect a non-performer has on other people, who feel like they're pulling all the weight.

Think of it as a poor fit rather than failure. The non-performer may just be in the wrong job. Try moving a low-performer into a job that's a better match for his talents. If that doesn't work, then it's probably not an issue of fit, it's an issue of the person's quality. In that case, cut your losses quickly.

You also have to distinguish between people who lack the ability or drive to deliver and those who fall short because they are taking appropriate risks. Exploring new markets, processes, products, or services is necessary to keep your company competitive, but such experiments may occasionally fail, when, for instance, the assumptions turn out to be wrong. That's different from taking reckless actions that were not thought through.

Manage the Intersections

If you're starting your leadership career, you might think the work of a corporate board of directors is far different from yours, but in fact some issues are the same at every organizational level. The business press is rife with stories of companies that ran aground because the board, which is ultimately in charge of appointing and removing the CEO, stood idle. In a surprising number of those cases, the board was star-studded. Individual members had proven records of accomplishment leading other large business organizations and stellar reputations for high integrity. These highly qualified individuals didn't take corrective action soon enough because they didn't work well *as a group*.

The stakes might be smaller, but your challenge to get people working well together is much the same. If you're in a position to choose the group and control the incentives, that's great. Even if you can't, you can practice this skill—managing the intersections—with any group you are part of.

Every sizable organization is divided into departments and/or business functions as well as geographic or business units. But a great deal of work gets done by people who exchange information across those organizational boundaries and collaborate on projects and decisions. To make cross-functional work happen more smoothly, some organizations have a matrix structure, in which people have multiple reporting relationships. Myriad software applications and online platforms exist to facilitate project management, knowledge sharing, and communication across time zones, but they can't ensure that individual efforts get integrated, and they surely don't overcome the human behavior that tends to get in the way.

That's where you come in. Think of yourself as an integrator, a term I use to describe leaders who are particularly good at getting diverse groups of people to coalesce. Integrators get people to see beyond the narrow view of their organizational silo or expertise by focusing on the bigger picture of what is best for the unit or company as a whole. It doesn't take formal authority to be an integrator. I've seen engineers and junior managers play that role. It takes skill in getting the best ideas and necessary facts on the table, helping the group shape alternatives, and keeping individuals focused on the common goal as they wrestle to make trade-offs and decisions.

Leaders who understand this role and play it skillfully will unleash tremendous energy. All of us have experienced the disappointment if not outright frustration of being involved in group work that doesn't go anywhere: people won't break from their entrenched opinions, trade-offs aren't made, some members don't meet their commitments or fail to show up. These and other common problems drain energy, time, and money. Given that one group's work is interconnected with others—the output from a product development team, for instance, affects what the marketing team and senior leaders can accomplish—any slowdown, failure to deliver, or toxicity spreads.

Helping groups function well has the opposite effect. The energy is contagious. Applied to the organization's most critical intersections—for example, among the CFO, CHRO, and chief strategy officer—skillful integration can energize the entire company. Recognizing the importance of integration, Sajan Pillai, CEO of UST Global, the multinational provider of IT services and solutions, created a new job category to do just that, and made it part of the track to become a senior leader. The new job began as a kind of experiment in 2012, when the company assigned nine people to the role, carefully chosen because they knew the company well, understood the business, knew a lot of people in the company, had a sense of urgency to execute things, and were sensitive to customers. Their explicit duty was to help knit the team together and identify whatever was getting in the way of accomplishing the goal. Sometimes it meant seeking help from an expert in another part of the company, or in one case, enlisting the help of a senior executive to close a sale that was teetering. Combining their social skills and business knowledge, they were able to make the right connections among people and clarify things, so results materialized faster. Morale went up as well, and in 2016 the company expanded its integrator ranks.

Lead the Dialogue

The essence of group work is in the dialogue. It's where behaviors are modeled, corrected, and reinforced. You may have spent time developing your presentation skills and gaining confidence to stand before a group with a PowerPoint deck. That skill won't go to waste, but it takes a different skill and arguably more confidence to shape a dialogue when you're in the middle of it. It's not something you can develop in isolation, as you would rehearse a speech. You practice in real situations. This is where leadership becomes a performing art, as you adjust the dialogue in real time, right there for all the group to see.

You know a great dialogue when you see one. People are mentally engaged, and might even lose track of time. They are respectful of one another but they don't hold back on what they really think. There's toughness to it, and informality. Points of disagreement and conflicting interests are not suppressed but are allowed to come to the surface. And new ideas emerge spontaneously. That's why someone like Mark Zuckerberg will pick up the phone and call a superstar business leader or technology guru and talk for an hour, and why Sunil Mittal, the founder of Bharti Airtel, the huge global telecom provider based in India, went to see the then-CEO of British Telecom when Mittal was a relative unknown. Conversation creates intellectual content, which is important to personal and business growth.

One reason people hate meetings is because of the dialogue that takes place. The conversation wanders, it's boring, and there's no conclusion to anything. If you learn the skill of conducting dialogue, you will find it to be a powerful leadership tool. Practice it wherever you go, with whomever you talk to, but be especially aware of how you use it to steer your team when they meet together.

In 2006, when Alan Mulally joined Ford Motor Company as CEO, the company was bleeding cash, and pressure was mounting as the other U.S. automakers were nearing bankruptcy, which would free them from their debt and allow them to price more aggressively. Ford had little time to fix its problems, and some observers had given up hope. Bill Ford, great grandson of Henry, had not. He stepped aside as CEO, clearing the way for Mulally to ply his leadership skills at Ford the way he had at Boeing. Mulally immediately took hold of the reins.

As he drilled to the root cause of Ford's problems, Mulally was convinced that the lack of information sharing and candid dialogue was crippling the company. Small problems were buried until they became enormous, poor performance went unchallenged, and you couldn't trust the numbers. While another leader might have made inspiring speeches about changing the culture, Mulally got to work to change the content and tone of the dialogue in weekly meetings of the senior team that he called business plan reviews, or BPRs.

He established the BPRs in his first week on the job and made attendance mandatory. The purpose was to track progress on the company's turnaround goals. Meetings were nothing new at Ford; in fact, Mulally disbanded a slew of them. But the ground rules for this meeting were far different. Each executive would report on his or her activities the previous week. The reports were expected to be succinct, honest, and fact-based. Executives had to speak for themselves without relying on subordinates leafing through three-ring binders. There was to be no side discussion or swiping, as was common before.

In his first BPR, Mulally laid out his vision for the company and set the expectation that the group would work as one unit in helping Ford regain its leadership. In subsequent BPRs, the dialogue made it clear that he meant business. The leaders captured progress on their operational targets in charts that were color-coded red, yellow, or green, and Mulally posted them around the room so everyone could see them. He focused on the reds and yellows, but he knew that if he blamed or embarrassed anyone for discussing their problems, they'd do everything they could to hide them.

So when Mark Fields, then head of the Americas at Ford (now CEO of Ford), admitted there was trouble with the launch of the Edge crossover vehicle, Mulally went the other way. He praised Fields's candor, then calmly asked the team, "Who can help Mark with this?" It was a pivotal moment. People made suggestions and offered resources.

There can be little doubt that Mulally's conduct of the dialogue influenced behavior.

As a leader, you influence the dialogue. It's up to you to use it as a tool. Don't let the conversation wander, half truths go unchecked, and piecemeal perspectives and politicking overtake the search for insights, solutions, and movement toward the common goal. Your direction of the dialogue makes all the difference.

Follow these guidelines to make meetings energizing and productive rather than an utter waste of time:

- Know your goal: What do you want to be accomplished by the end?

- Know your intention: How do you want to shape behavior?

- Press for the truth, good or bad.

- Really listen, including for what is *not* being said.

- Develop and clarify ideas and options.

- Bring conflict to the open and resolve it.

- Bring the meeting to closure: Who will do what, by when?

Be a Social Architect

Earlier I stressed the importance of integrating perspectives and activities at critical intersections. Many of these intersections are defined by the organization chart, but particularly as the scope of your responsibilities expands, you will have an opportunity to be the "social architect" who identifies and defines them. It is never too soon to practice seeing the organization through this lens. The organization will perform faster and better if you understand where people need to come together to make important decisions, design the organization accordingly, and diagnose how well those intersections are working.

The way to identify important intersections is to think about the expected outputs. Say you have a major goal of introducing a series of new products in the next three years. Decisions about which ideas to fund and develop are critical. Who needs to be involved in making those decisions, and how will they come together? You have to define who will participate, who will be accountable, and what information must be brought to bear. You would want to include people who have deep knowledge of consumers, for example, and perhaps someone who can help secure financial resources. You might want people who understand important geographic markets, a top-notch technologist who usually works alone in a lab, or an expert in data analytics. All the critical people needed to make progress should be together in the room, but don't pad the group or include people just to assuage their egos.

Knowing that every group needs a leader, you should be unambiguous about who is responsible for integrating the work at this intersection and actually making timely, high-quality decisions. Don't defer to hierarchy. Assign someone who is a skilled integrator.

Once you've identified the important intersections and perhaps designed some new ones, don't just turn away. You have to continually keep them in your sights to ensure that they are functioning well. A simple diagnostic checklist can help:

- Does this group have the information they need, including from outside the company?

- Is there a power imbalance?

- Do they have the resources they need?

- Are conflicts being resolved?

- Are the incentives right?

- If they're not moving forward, is there an energy drainer who should be removed from the group? And is this is still the right leader?

When people are working well together at critical intersections, decisions are made, work gets done, and results materialize. Individuals are more productive and more satisfied. The release of energy is exponential.

How Tony Palmer Became a Talent Magnet

When he was twenty-one years old, Tony Palmer, now president of global brands and innovation at Kimberly-Clark, wasn't sure he would get into college, let alone rise to the executive ranks of a major corporation. The son of a sheep shearer who traveled around Australia's Outback, he attended junior school by correspondence and didn't quite graduate high school. But he had the drive to keep learning and to create his own path. That drive was on full display in Melbourne in those early days, when he sat on the steps of a college every day for three weeks until finally the dean stopped to ask him what he wanted. Palmer explained his desire to be a student but that he did not have a high school diploma, and the dean suggested he apply as a "nontraditional student." He did, and was accepted.

Was it hard being three years older than the typical freshman? "I had an unfair advantage in college," Palmer told me, "because I really wanted to be there. I worked harder than everybody else, and did very well academically."

Fresh out of college three years later, he worked for a consulting firm, received an MBA from IMD in Switzerland, took a marketing job at Mars Australia, and rather than move to the United States to take a step up the ladder at Mars, he leapt to a job at a sugar company in Australia. "The next step at Mars was not going to further my knowledge or improve me at all, so I went to what was probably a lesser company for a job that had a much broader brief," Palmer said. "It was a really tough business situation that was going to be very difficult to turn around, but it gave me the chance to do something different and test my skills."

Among the challenges at the sugar company was managing people. "I had five people reporting to me who had about 140 years of combined experience," Palmer says. "I was just thirty-two, and I was their boss. I had no choice but to overcome my discomfort and take charge, and through some smart marketing, we improved the profitability of the business enormously."

That job was part of a pattern in Palmer's life: taking on big challenges, later at Coca-Cola, Fisher Scientific, Kellogg, and now at Kimberly-Clark, and forming his views on leading people. "If I were to go back to when I was younger, I probably wouldn't like myself very much," Palmer says candidly, "because it was a lot about me and what I was going to do in my career. As I've gone through my career, I've come to the point where I define myself by helping other people be successful. I've learned that when other people succeed at work, it really does improve their lives at home and more generally, because they're happier and they have a good time. It's a really powerful thing, and I get a lot of enjoyment out of that."

When Palmer was at the sugar company, people from other companies got to know him through negotiations, and Coca-Cola recruited him to their Minute Maid brand in the United States. Palmer says, "When I was offered the job by Sergio Zyman, who was chief marketing officer, I had never even been to the U.S. I was excited but terrified of packing up alone and moving to a country I'd never visited. But Sergio took a bet on me. It was a very big deal to me and very eye-opening. And I learned a ton through that process.

"I felt compelled to understand why he'd offered me the job," Palmer continued, "so I picked up the phone and asked. I said, 'Sergio, don't get me wrong; I want the job. But why would you choose somebody who has never worked in the U.S.? I'm sure there are a hundred people there who know the business better than I do. Why have you chosen me?'

"I'll never forget Sergio's response. He said, 'I'll choose an athlete with a dream over a person doing a job any day.' Sergio can be very hard on people. But if he sees talent, he'll back you and give you an opportunity. And it was a life-changing opportunity for me."

After several years, Palmer felt he could no longer make an impact at Coke and took a job as president of private label manufacturing for Fisher Scientific. It was owned by a private equity group that didn't see people the way Palmer did. "It was all about the numbers and winning at all costs," Palmer says. "When I realized that, I started looking for a different job."

He landed at Kellogg, where he put his evolving views of people into practice and cemented a reputation as a talent magnet, as his boss wrote in his performance review. "I gained conviction about wanting to improve people's lives by helping them win in business," Palmer says. "So when I think about people for our business, I consider the whole person, not just the business elements. There's a tendency for everybody to ask what the person can do for the business. When I interview someone, whether they're coming from inside or outside the business, my first questions are What's your dream? What do you want to achieve personally and professionally?

"That enables you to understand what they're looking for and then to try and match it to the business. But I always start with the person. And I'm open with them about that—hey, if we can't meet your dreams, why would you come here? It's a waste of time. Let's talk about that first and then decide whether we should keep talking."

Palmer was happy running the UK and Ireland for Kellogg, their biggest market outside the United States, when he was offered the chance to make another big leap by moving to Kimberly-Clark. "People thought I was crazy to take it," Palmer explains, "because I was going from a big line job to a staff job in marketing at KC. But I'd met Tom Falk, the CEO, through a recruiter I had a long-term relationship with, and I was convinced he was a great leader. I bought into his vision, and it was an opportunity to do something on a scale that I wasn't going to get elsewhere."

At KC Palmer continued to hone his skills as a talent magnet. "I've spent a lot of time at KC developing a network of people we might be interested in recruiting in the future, even if we don't have jobs right now. I personally call them and have a conversation about what their dreams are, what they want to do, and I tell them about our business. Right now I have a file of probably forty people, mostly general managers, and I'm actually doing R&D at the moment. Then it's just continuous follow-up with those people over time, so if I'm in London or somewhere, I'll grab a cup of coffee with somebody. It takes just a half hour to sit down and talk, and it's how you get to know them. Then when a job does come up, you've got this list of qualified people you can tap."

Who, then, do you choose? Palmer counts technical competence as just a ticket to play. "There are plenty of people in the organization who know about marketing or know about supply chain or whatever. I interview people for leadership ability," Palmer says. "I look for five things. First is learning agility. Second is cultural acuity, which I define as being able to put yourself in different situations or have a difference of opinion with somebody and work your way through it. Third is the ability to make things happen without direct authority over people, fourth is desire or how hungry you are, and fifth is whether you can develop talent. I ask questions around those things to get a holistic view of the person's leadership competence." Palmer also spends about half his time coaching people, mostly on leadership competence.

"I've done a lot of things in business—whether it's fixing the portfolio or the supply chain or improving marketing—but leading people is really important in my life," Palmer concludes. "To me, talent extraction and development is a matter of discipline, not a gift you're given. It takes discipline and work. But when you go out of your way to help other people, it gives you a good feeling and it's amazing how it comes back to you and the business in unusual ways."

Hipo Coaching Checklist – Chapter 3

Multiply the Energy and Skills of Those Around You

- Set aside time on your calendar to regularly practice your skill in judging and developing other people's talents.
- Remember the formula for building high-performing teams:
  - People Quality + Job Fit + Collaboration = Team Performance

☐ **1. Identify a Person's God-Given Talent**
  - What is the person really good at? Go beyond the quantitative data and your first impressions.
  - Talk with the person.
  - Ask what he or she enjoys. What inspires him? How he makes decisions. How he achieves results.
  - Invite her to lunch, meet socially or find ways to interact outside of the usual business environment. If you get to know her in a variety of settings, you will have far more insight into her.
  - Carefully observe the person's decisions and behaviors.
  - Look back on past decisions the person has made:
    - Consider the quality of the decisions, and also the methodology used.
    - Did he leap to conclusions or get bogged down in analysis?
    - Did he use judgment versus strictly relying on numerical facts? That will help you see the degree to which he is an intuitive thinker and how much risk he's willing to take.
  - Meetings are a good chance to observe behaviors:
    - How does he handle disagreements?
    - Does she listen to opposing views and try to find common ground or dig in her heels?
    - Does he share information willingly?

- Does she come up with creative solutions?
- Does he elicit negative or positive behavior from others?
- Consider their networks. Do they have diverse social networks or participate in groups that expose them to a range of perspectives?
- Skip the negatives for a moment, and think only about the positives.
- In two or three clear sentences, using simple everyday language, how would you describe this person?
- To sharpen your observational skills and avoid unconscious bias, cross-check your observations with others.
- Ask them to state in clear, simple sentences a few specific positives about the person:
  - Ask for specific examples of how the person makes decisions or gets results.
  - Note any differences that emerge, and use those insights as something to watch for and explore further.

☐ **2. Build Other People's Strengths**
- After you identify where a person's natural abilities lie, think of creative ways to build on those abilities. This should be an ongoing everyday activity for every hipo.
- If you have a large number of people reporting to you, focus on those who are in the most influential jobs, but also keep a watchful eye for others who have high potential.
- Talk with each person frequently about his or her strengths, and how they could be better leveraged in the organization.
- If your company hasn't already moved away from annual performance reviews to the more effective weekly or monthly performance feedback meetings, set them up yourself.
- Create your own routine for providing direct, honest feedback, the more frequently the better.
- In addition to your predominant focus on their strengths, also include constructive feedback. Choose one or two things the person should focus on, and be clear and specific. It could be a particular business skill the person needs to acquire, or it could be on the behavior side. Focus on specific skills or behaviors they could develop more fully, or actions you would like to see them take in the future.
- At least quarterly, consider the job he or she has now and how it might be reshaped, or whether another job would be more effective in allowing the person to excel.
- Remember that the best way to engage a person's energy and boost performance is the personal attention you give to helping him or her leverage and grow his or her talents.

(continued)

(continued)

☐ **3. Make Necessary Changes Quickly**
  • If someone on your team isn't delivering results, move quickly.
  • Meet with the person and honestly present the facts. Ask for insights on how the problem can be fixed.
  • If you need feedback from others, gather it objectively. Ask for specific facts—not opinions, accusations, or complaints. Then ask if they have any potential solutions for getting the person back on track.
  • Be sure to distinguish between people who lack the ability or drive to deliver and those who fall short because they are taking appropriate risks.
  • If there's a problem that can be fixed by additional training, move quickly to make that happen.
  • If the problem is with the person-job fit, can you find a better match for the person's skills in another role or another part of the company?
  • If moving the person into another role doesn't work, then it's probably not an issue of fit, it's an issue of the person's quality. In that case, cut your losses quickly.
  • Throughout the process, work with your HR team to ensure that all company and legal guidelines are met.
  • When hiring a new person to fill the role, don't be afraid to hire someone better than you. That's how you'll build the high-performing team you need.

☐ **4. Manage the Intersections**
  • Look for opportunities to exchange information across silos and collaborate on projects and decisions that transcend organizational boundaries.
  • Think of yourself as an integrator, and help people see beyond the narrow view of their organizational silo or expertise by focusing on the bigger picture of what is best for the unit or company as a whole.
  • Practice this skill continually. The better you become at getting diverse groups of people to coalesce, the more effective you will be as a leader and the better prepared you will be for a more senior role.
  • It doesn't take formal authority to be an integrator; it just takes intention and practice.

☐ **5. Lead the Dialogue**
  • The effectiveness of every interaction depends on the quality of its dialogue. That's where behaviors are modeled, corrected, and reinforced.

- Your challenge is to adjust the dialogue, in real time, to keep it directed toward positive results.
- If the conversation wanders, bring it back to the point. Don't let half-truths go unchecked or piecemeal perspectives and politicking take over the dialogue. Keep all parties focused on the search for insights, solutions, and movement toward the common goal.
- Practice this wherever you go, with whomever you talk, but be especially aware of how you use it to steer your team when they meet.
- One effective practice is to have each team member report on his or her activities the previous week. Expect them to be succinct, honest, and fact-based. If anyone is facing a problem, praise the person for candor and ask the team, "Who can help with this?"
- You'll know that you're leading good dialogues when people are mentally engaged. They're respectful of one another but don't hold back on what they really think. There's toughness to the conversation, and informality. Points of disagreement and conflicting interests are not suppressed but are allowed to come to the surface. There's an underlying commitment to a common goal, and each person understands how he or she can contribute.

☐ **6. Make Your Meetings Effective**
- Know your goal: what do you want to be accomplished by the end?
- Know your intention: how do you want to shape behavior?
- Really listen, including for what is *not* being said.
- Steer the conversation: keep it on track, focused on insights and solutions, and moving toward a common goal.
- Develop and clarify ideas and options.
- Bring conflict into the open.
- Bring the meeting to closure: who will do what, by when?

☐ **7. Be a Social Architect**
- As you expand your ability to manage the intersections and become more skilled at integrating perspectives and activities at critical connection points, this may earn you a new opportunity—the chance to become a "social architect" who identifies and defines new intersections.
- It is never too soon to practice seeing the organization through this lens, especially as more and more companies are changing their business models and organizational structures in response to increasing digitization and global footprints.

(continued)

(continued)

- You can identify important intersections by thinking about the expected outputs:
  - What does the organization want to achieve?
  - What decisions need to be made to make that happen?
  - Who needs to be involved in making those decisions, and how will they come together?
  - Who will participate, who will be accountable, and what information must be brought to bear?
- Don't pad the group or include people just to assuage their egos, but make sure all the critical people needed to make progress are together in the room.
- After you understand where people need to come together to make important decisions, design the organization accordingly and diagnose how well those intersections are working.
- When bringing a new group together, continually keep them in your sights to ensure that they are functioning well. A simple diagnostic checklist can help:
  - Does this group have the information they need, including from outside the company?
  - Is there a power imbalance?
  - Do they have the resources they need?
  - Are conflicts being resolved?
  - Are the incentives right?
  - If they're not moving forward, is there an energy drainer who should be removed from the group?
  - And is this still the right leader?

NOTE: Now is a good time to reassess your goals. If you don't enjoy developing people, providing frequent positive and constructive feedback, and leading effective dialogues, you may want to consider reorienting your focus on building your skills as a high-potential individual contributor instead of a high-potential leader. High-potential individuals would be losing ground if they set their sights on a job where they have to deal with a never-ending stream of people and relationship issues that they have little interest in. There's no shortage of great opportunities for talented individuals.

Additional Resources

Charan, Ram, Steve Drotter, and Jim Noel. *The Leadership Pipeline: How to Build the Leadership Powered Company.* San Francisco, CA: John Wiley & Sons, Inc., 2011.

Comaford, Christine. "Why Performance Management Is Dead and Performance Motivation Is Here to Stay." *Forbes.com*. October 22, 2016. http://www.forbes.com/sites/christinecomaford/2016/10/22/why-performance-management-is-dead-performance-motivation-is-here-to-stay/print/.

Conaty, Bill, and Ram Charan. *The Talent Masters: Why Smart Leaders Put People Before Numbers*. New York: Crown Publishing Group, 2010.

Rath, Tom. *StrengthsFinder 2.0*. New York: Gallup Press, 2007.

4

Be a Master of Big Ideas and Execution

If you're a hipo, you're naturally inclined to look at the organization from the outside in. Like most of your fellow millennials, you live on the Internet, message boards, websites, and social networks. What differentiates you from your age-mates is that you're able to use that information to come up with ideas that could create a new market, a new competitive advantage, a new game, or even change the world. The ability to satisfy your curiosity twenty-four hours a day with total access to information is a great spur to creativity, but your ideas must be actionable. To see your vision come to life, you have to be disciplined in shaping the ideas, deciding which ones to pursue, and converting them into specific actions so they can be executed in a way that delivers results. True hipos can do both: come up with big ideas and get them executed.

Make Your Big Ideas Better

The transparency and democratization that are creeping into the workplace are a gift to hipos who have big ideas and want to be heard. Senior leaders at many legacy companies are realizing that you don't need decades of experience and high organizational status to generate great ideas. Long tenure can in fact be a detriment when it comes to conceiving something radically new. They've begun to search for ideas for growth and transformation across the organization, by soliciting e-mails addressed to them personally from anyone in the company, setting up intracompany discussion boards, inviting younger employees to brainstorming sessions, or creating contests or hackathons. It's common now for CEOs to encourage the team to listen to the millennials they work with, if only because they represent the perspective of digital natives.

You should feel encouraged to put your ideas out there, but they are more likely to gain traction if you develop your skill in shaping and reshaping them first. Most great ideas start as one thing but are reshaped in iterations to make them better.

The best way to clarify your ideas—whether they have to do with a new product, a new way of competing, a new way of working with ecosystem partners, or a new technology platform—is by talking with others. That's why you hear about entrepreneurs striking up conversations with other businesspeople and technologists, and why some companies send teams off to places like Singularity University, the technology- and future-focused think tank based in Silicon Valley, for brainstorming sessions facilitated by third parties. Even if you become top dog, you will want to do this. I've seen many CEOs test their ideas and refine their thinking by conferring with colleagues, board members, and friends who are experienced businesspeople, consultants, or investment bankers.

How to Assess Your Good Ideas

Most millennials understand the value of creating a minimum viable product that is tested, rejiggered, and tested again. Some products can go through several iterations in a matter of weeks. The idea of going through iterations applies to business ideas in general, such as how the company is positioned in the marketplace or ecosystem, as well as products. You don't necessarily need elaborate charts or a formalized plan to present your idea, but you need crystal-clear thinking about how and why it will work and make a positive impact on the business.

For many products, the toughest issue is not whether the idea can be made practical but whether it can be scaled up, brought to market properly, and deliver financial results. You should be able to answer a set of questions such as these:

1. Who is the customer? How will it change the customer's end-to-end experience, digital or non-digital? Will it substitute an existing experience? Will customers find it compelling? Will it require a change in the customer's habit? Many millennials are eager to develop new customer experiences using algorithms, social media, video, and the like, without thinking things through from the customer's perspective. Taking the customer's view, not just the technologist's, was one of Steve Jobs's great strengths.

2. Can the idea be converted into a platform? What will it take to do so? By platform, I mean the set of algorithms at the center of a reconceived or newly created ecosystem in which various parties participate to deliver the customer experience. Amazon, for example, is a platform that connects a range of vendors with consumers using algorithms to ease the search for relevant products and to facilitate their delivery.

3. What will it take to scale up fast? You have to know what capabilities and resources will be required and have ideas about how to get them.

4. What competition can you expect, and how would you deal with it? Will your idea provoke a response from a giant like Amazon, Netflix, or Google? Would a small born-digital player suddenly displace you? Consider the second-, third-, and maybe even fourth-order consequences.

5. What funding are you going to need? If you want to obtain funding from inside, you have to understand what your

company's gatekeepers will be looking for beyond the qualitative stuff. For example, when will it show a positive return on investment? How much capital is needed? And what are the risks?

6. What will prevent you from succeeding? You will gain a lot of confidence and win others over by thinking about what bottlenecks and barriers you might encounter and how to deal with them.

The questions will differ for non-product ideas, but the theme is constant: above all else, the idea must be mentally tested. Say you have an idea to expand into an area where the company doesn't yet compete. Questions to help you fully develop your idea might include:

1. What would your idea actually look like if it were to become reality? Vision is a word often associated with entrepreneurs, meaning that their idea is very big and long term. They picture something in their minds that others don't see. CNN founder Ted Turner imagined news being televised nationally twenty-four hours a day when cable TV was in its infancy. Bill Gates imagined a computer on every desk in the era of costly mainframes and mini computers. Actual drawing, sketches, and diagrams may convey your idea better than words, and it will force you to be specific and concrete. You've probably heard people talk about ideas that began on the back of a napkin. I heard a firsthand account from Harvey Koeppel, the former chief information officer (CIO) of Citigroup's Global Consumer Group, who told me how the bank's entry into mobile banking began. One day he was in India visiting branches that had adopted the latest technology, and he noticed how much customers liked using it. That evening, sitting with an Indian manager, he wondered aloud if the same services could be done on

a mobile device. Soon the two of them were excitedly sketching out the application on a napkin, and it was launched three months later.

2. What are the five or six building blocks you would need to have in place to make that idea a reality? For example, would it require new technical or marketing capabilities? How would you build or acquire them? Sunil Mittal built his India-based telecom powerhouse Bharti Airtel in part by creatively solving the problem of financial and capabilities constraints. He had entered the Indian telecom space at its infancy, and as demand for mobile phone service exploded, his start-up was going toe to toe against major industrial companies with deep pockets. His solution was to outsource the entire delivery system to companies like IBM, Ericsson, and Motorola, which expanded along with him. It reduced his need for capital and freed him to focus sharply on growing the customer base.

3. How will this idea make money? Hipos understand the universal principles of money making, such as revenues (sales), gross margin (sales minus the costs directly related to the product or service), velocity (also known as inventory turns), and cash flow. These measures exist in every country and in every size business, from a sole proprietorship to a giant conglomerate. Money making may not be immediate, but what's the time frame? Creating a digital platform is a drain on cash and profits, because you probably have to hire expensive talent to build it. How long will the added expense of high salaries be a drain on cash and profits? Where will the cash come from, and how will other parts of the business be affected?

4. What changes in the external environment would make this idea succeed better? What would make it fail? These might include actions by governmental bodies. The precursor

to Ted Turner's nationwide twenty-four-hour cable news channel was a change in how the Federal Communications Commission granted broadcast licenses. Previously, licenses had to be secured one by one in local jurisdictions. He argued that granting national licenses through one application would expand consumer choice, and the FCC eventually bought in to that argument. That regulatory change cleared the path for Turner to quickly build a national network transmitted through satellites and cables from the tiny local station he owned and laid the groundwork for CNN.

5. What are the most critical hurdles you would have to overcome to bring this idea to fruition? It may be a matter of making a technical breakthrough, or a regulatory one, or winning over an important constituency.

6. Is this the right time? The way to be sure you're not too early or too late is by talking with people. Can they see the need? Do they support you? Watch your biases; while they may have allowed you to spot an opportunity, they could as easily block you from seeing potential issues down the road. Allow yourself to hear the negatives, then you can try to address them.

Executing Big Ideas

Dreaming is fine, but converting lofty ideas into results is the acid test of high potential. Understanding the ins and outs of execution will help you turn ideas into reality, and ensure that your ideas are grounded in the first place. Don't be afraid to toss out the bad ideas. Better ones will come.

Execution is a discipline all its own; in fact, I wrote an entire book about it with Larry Bossidy, the former CEO of Honeywell. It is a hands-on activity for every leader, not the dirty work you can delegate to someone else while you think big thoughts. You will have to master it to get results, and the truth is, it will improve the quality of your business thinking.

The heart of getting things executed well lies in how you work within three core processes that every company has in one form or another: for managing people, strategy, and operations. You have to be involved in all three areas, get information and real dialogue going in them, and recognize the connections among them. Big-picture strategic thinking, for example, is useless unless it takes into account the human capacity you have in terms of the number of people and their skills. Are your software engineers up to speed on algorithms and data analytics if that's the direction you're headed? Operational realities must also be factored into whatever direction you are taking the business. Can you expand manufacturing capacity fast enough to keep pace with the new growth initiative, and do you have the resources to do it? Ideas not linked to practical realities at the ground level are doomed to fail.

Even if your current job is narrow in scope, you can learn to see the interconnections among people, strategy, and operations and bring that broader perspective to bear in your daily work. You might be the one to point out that the boss's great plan will require hiring three more people, something the budget doesn't account for, or that the earnings needed to fund growth might not materialize unless the company shores up its capabilities in negotiating with big suppliers.

Keep those interconnections in mind as you break your big idea into specific action items. What has to happen, by when? Maybe you'll need to build a whole new team of people with skills in data analytics and algorithms. How fast does that have to happen, and does something else have to happen first? Shifting resources is a particular dilemma for many companies that are trying to become digital centered. For example, they may need to spend heavily on expertise needed to build a digital platform, while ensuring their existing products or business don't fall behind the competition.

The pacing and sequence are crucial. Be clear about how your ideas fit with and improve upon current operating plans.

Timing is also critical in entering new geographic markets, as are the linkages among strategy, operations, and people. Is it important to have a critical mass in place at once, or is it something to be gradually developed? KFC slowed its initial entry to China until it knew it would have a cadre of people capable of managing the restaurants.

Good leaders seek input from people close to the ground and adjust for those realities as they define the specific actions that need to be taken, and their timing. Then they assign specific goals, and follow through to make sure the work gets done and results materialize.

Execution Basics

Bossidy once offered this brief but powerful piece of leadership advice: you have to show up. What he meant was that you have to be visible, present, and mentally engaged with the people whose efforts you oversee and coordinate. You have to stay in touch to know what they're actually doing and drive accountability through your behavior and actions. Leaders who are good at execution do that through three particular actions:

1. **Set clear goals and priorities.** As a hipo, you may be naturally inclined to see the world from a high-level perspective and in all its complexity. But you have to be able to crystallize the five or six things that really matter, not just for yourself, as discussed in Chapter 2, but for those who report to you. Saying that everything is important is like saying nothing really is. It's not helpful. Use your mental skill to sift, sort, and select the things that matter most and have some urgency to them, and be explicit about what each person is supposed to be working on. If you struggle to go

from the clouds to the ground level, get some coaching from people who have done it before. It's a skill you can develop.

Make the assignments, and establish some milestones, so you will be able to measure progress instead of waiting for the goal to be complete. What has to be accomplished by when? The milestones could be qualitative, for example, identifying three potential new suppliers in Southeast Asia or developing alternative paths for entering a new market.

2. **Stay informed about how things are going.** Execution demands that you create a means to stay informed, whether it's a weekly meeting like the business plan reviews Alan Mulally used as CEO of Ford (see Chapter 3), or a biweekly check-in with phone calls and personal visits in between. When the stakes are high and speed is paramount, daily contact may be best. You can't afford to wait for problems to come to you; by talking to people often, you'll discover them sooner and can address them before they get out of hand. Frequency of contact is important, but so is your willingness to ask hard questions and search below the surface, for example, to get to the root of why progress is slowing. Has the person lost energy or interest? Why? Maybe there is an unresolved conflict in the organization or a toxic personality in the mix.

   Your behavior has everything to do with whether or not information reaches you without distortion. If you shoot the messenger, word gets around and the information channels shut down. Focus on the business problem at hand, and try to work *with* the person to identify and overcome problems in converting ideas into action. If solutions don't emerge, make a plan to generate some.

3. **Follow through and follow up.** Clarity about who is doing what, by when, sets the stage for accountability; frequent check-ins help keep things moving forward; but you also

have to be clear about what is okay and what is not. When it comes to accountability, actions speak louder than words. You have to reinforce the positives, for example, by rewarding the doers, the ones who overcome the problems and deliver results, with praise, support, and promotions and financial rewards when appropriate. In doing so, you will increase the psychological energy and motivation not just for that person but also for everybody else. Bossidy's business reviews were conducted in the spirit of making progress and delivering results, and they could be hard hitting. To make sure people knew what was expected, he followed up with a memo summarizing the outcomes of the meeting. He didn't want people to feel demoralized by constructive criticism, so he also made a habit of writing personal notes that reinforced his confidence in the person.

At the same time, if someone fails to deliver repeatedly, you have to face the issue head-on. Start with a one-on-one conversation, where you don't sugarcoat the feedback, and if the person doesn't improve, you might have to put someone else in the job. Allowing non-performers to slide drains everybody's energy and puts your own job at risk.

Ask Incisive Questions

Asking the right questions will help you gauge other people's performance and unearth problems in execution. Most of us are trained to give answers, not ask questions, but this is a valuable skill. A side benefit is to better anticipate and answer questions that are asked of you. How often have you worked hard on a presentation, then were hit by a single question you weren't prepared for?

You learn this art by watching others who are good at it, as you would an artist or craftsman. Try this: in any review or meeting, make note of the questions that are asked, not the answers.

Consumer research, teaching by the case method, boardroom discussions, and analyst calls—all rely heavily on questions. As you observe, you will begin to see that most questions are used many times. The best questions are brief and cut through the clutter to a pivotal assumption or bigger point. The tone is respectful, not insulting or fear-inducing.

Good questions create order out of a jumble of information and condition your mind. Try it on yourself. When you are preparing a presentation or meeting, start with the most critical questions you need to answer. That orients your thinking, and you will be more to the point.

If you have a thoughtful set of questions you ask of others, you will begin to condition their minds. Say you're hoping to launch a pilot product by a certain date, and the team has missed the milestones at least three times. Needless to say, you've heard all the excuses. If your line of questioning is consistent, people will start to anticipate what you are likely to ask and may take actions to address the problems ahead of time.

A Hipo's Vision and Execution at Fingerhut

Love Goel is the billionaire founder and CEO of GVG Capital, which invests in companies that are undergoing digital transformation. Goel, who built a dozen big e-commerce companies and is sometimes referred to as the father of multi-channel retailing, has been featured in the *The Wall Street Journal*, *Fortune*, and *Barron's*. Most recently, he partnered with the board and management team of B2W Digital in Brazil to lead its turnaround, building it into Latin America's largest e-commerce company and generating billions for its shareholders.

Back in the 1990s, Goel was a hipo, a smart but untested twenty-something IT guy with an insatiable drive "to learn and do everything." When he was recruited by Fingerhut, a fifty-year-old catalog retailer based in Minnesota, it proved to be the perfect environment for him to pursue big ideas and have them executed. Until it wasn't, and he had to move on.

In his early twenties, Goel worked at Apple, Cargill, Prudential, Sears, and Deloitte, where he was working when Alan Bignall, the CIO of Fingerhut, recruited him as head of technology strategy and architecture. Goel says, "Alan saw something in me that he thought could be useful, and he was persuasive about the opportunity, saying there's this new thing called e-commerce, and Fingerhut has the best direct marketing platform in the country."

Fingerhut's expertise in selling directly to consumers was legendary. It attracted a steady stream of praise and of visitors eager to learn. It also had a huge IT budget—8 percent of its $2 billion in sales compared with the average 2 percent in retail. The company had, in fact, overspent to expand its call center, fulfillment center, and IT departments, and they wanted Goel to rein in costs or monetize the capacity it had not yet grown into.

Goel immediately set to work trimming IT costs, and the senior team took notice of his energy and expertise. In his first few months on the job, they summoned him to a meeting and made a request. They had heard that USSB (now DirecTV) was looking for bids to supply back office services; it would sell merchandise on its TV station and wanted another company to handle the work of getting the products to the consumer. Although Fingerhut had never provided that kind of a service before, they wondered if it might be a way to use some of its excess capacity, and wanted Goel to look into it.

The clock was ticking on the proposal deadline, so Goel quickly gathered a team of in-house experts and, after a four-hour session, reported back that the contract might be worth as much as $100 million. The top leaders were intrigued and asked Goel and his team to explore the issue a little more. Immediately.

"We started making phone calls, crunching numbers, and doing all kinds of research and analysis," Goel says. "By midnight, we understood what the project would entail, and it was bigger than any of us thought, about a billion dollars over five years."

Goel found the idea of landing a billion-dollar contract more enticing than intimidating. "I knew it was ambitious," Goel continued. "And there were twenty-four companies bidding on this, including major ones like EDS and Accenture, who did this kind of thing all the time. But the more we analyzed it, the more convinced I was that we could do it better than anybody else."

It was after midnight when Goel called the COO of the company. "Sorry to wake you up this late," he began, "but this is a billion dollar contract, and it's due in three days, and everyone and their brother is bidding on it."

The COO replied, "Okay, I'm going to call a special meeting of the board and the management committee tomorrow morning. I'd like your team to come in and present what you think we should do."

Goel came to the meeting exuding confidence, but others were skeptical. They reminded him that his team had no experience doing this, and that perhaps they should find a smaller project to bid on. "Everything they said was rational," Goel explains. "But working overnight, we had come up with a thesis. Delivering on this proposal would be difficult, but we had amazing capabilities. At the core, we had the richest and deepest customer database in America with 3,000 data points on thirty-two million consumers, and 1,500 data points on 100 million households. This enabled us to have the best call center in the country with the highest cross-sell and up-sell rates, the best and largest direct-to-consumer delivery capability, the best customer analytics and direct marketing capability, and expertise in managing inventory for this type of channel, which no one else had."

Goel's high energy and certainty were compelling, and so was the fact that he had already started to deliver the hoped-for cost reduction in IT. The senior team gave him a green light to submit the bid, and Fingerhut won it. Now the company needed the infrastructure to support the work, and the senior team gave Goel that responsibility, too. In less than two years, this business became the world's largest e-fulfillment business, helping Walmart launch its e-commerce business and Levi's sell its first pair of jeans online.

Bigger Than Amazon

Still within months of Goel joining the company, the head of marketing reached out to him, saying, "We've got this small $5 million e-commerce business and I'm not satisfied. How big do you think it can be?" Goel did an off-site with the e-commerce team and discovered they had "every single issue you can imagine." But there were lots of talented people, and Fingerhut had great assets—everything they needed to build a large e-commerce business. "I knew it could be bigger," Goel said. "I just didn't know how big."

He was put in charge, and off went the team to do a moonshot exercise, where he asked everyone to forget their preconceptions. Given everything we know about the external world and our internal assets, he told them, think about how big a business we could build if everything worked out perfectly.

This was shortly after Jeff Bezos had registered Amazon as the name of his business and had just recently moved out of the cramped basement where they had been fulfilling orders. Many people saw e-commerce as a novelty or fad.

Goel saw no reason why Fingerhut shouldn't have the biggest e-commerce business in the world. "We had a collection of some of the smartest people in direct marketing," Goel said. "People talk about algorithms today, but we had some of the original algorithm makers. They had figured out targeting, cross-selling, up-selling, all this better than anybody.

"What I had was the vision," he continued. "I saw the potential in doing all this, and I had an obsessive desire to get things done."

He also understood what it would take from a capital perspective and asked for $10 million to grow the business at least ten times bigger in twelve months. When they got to ten times far sooner than expected, he stepped back to rethink the whole thing.

"Suddenly I could see what we could build," Goel said. "It crystallized in my mind that we needed a technology platform, which is something that didn't exist anywhere in the world at the time, because nobody had built an e-commerce company at scale."

The CEO entrusted him to work with people outside Fingerhut to help him achieve the vision. He made a pitch to Dave Duffield and Larry Ellison, creators of PeopleSoft and Oracle, respectively, the two largest enterprise software companies, suggesting they build the software Fingerhut needed. Fingerhut had built great proprietary systems over fifty years for processing consumer orders by phone, mail, or fax, which had made it the largest and most profitable catalog retailer in America. Goel offered to share the intellectual property from those systems and back-end processes in exchange for the platform Fingerhut needed, which the software makers could later sell to other companies. The companies went to work, giving Fingerhut a digital platform ahead of everybody else, and saving it more than $60 million in capital expenditures.

By 1999, Fingerhut and its network of companies had the largest e-commerce business in the world. Bigger than Amazon.

From there, the vision kept getting bigger and bigger, as Goel and his team saw practically unlimited potential to create e-commerce websites for all sorts of categories—the world's first custom jewelry site, first flower site, first daily deals site, first credit-based site selling products on installments, and first sites for consumers of different income levels. "We realized we could execute these better than any other company and scale up fast," Goel says. "The pace was frenetic, because the opportunities were so endless."

The team learned to sort through the many ideas that bombarded them, and then created a venture capital arm to invest in ones they couldn't start themselves and that leveraged Fingerhut's assets. Goel helped build this venture capital arm, too, integrating almost two dozen digital businesses.

The Failure of Vision

Every hipo has to face the fact that a clear vision, well-thought-out plan, and even track record of executing well may not be enough to win the support you need. In 1999, Federated Department Stores (since rebranded as Macy's) bought Fingerhut, making it one of eight entities in its portfolio, along with Bloomingdale's and Macy's. New people controlled the resources, using different governing mechanisms.

Every month the top four people from Federated paid a visit, and the senior executive team from Fingerhut made a presentation, which was usually delivered by Goel. In August, the budgeting cycle began, and Goel requested $150 million in capital expenditures, which was less than the $168 million in free cash flow generated by Fingerhut and its network of digital businesses. "We're building the world's largest Internet business," he explained. "The Internet is going to be huge. Amazon, AOL, Netscape, Yahoo—they're all spending like a drunken sailor."

Federated's top brass would not agree to more than $50 million.

In September, Goel and his colleagues gave it another shot. Still there was disagreement.

As the October review approached, Fingerhut CEO Will Lansing said he wanted to make the presentation on his own, though, of course he welcomed input. He spent a lot of time preparing, and the day of the meeting he made a deeply emotional presentation about what Fingerhut had accomplished and where they wanted to take the company. "He poured his heart out for a full hour," Goel recalls, "and afterward, the room was silent. The Federated executives are savvy people. They knew the tension was high.

"Then the Federated CFO, who had failed to grasp the situation, jumped in. Instead of saying thank you for the heartfelt presentation, or let's see how we can make this happen, she asked a stupid question about a particular number in one of the financial statements. And I knew right then we weren't going anywhere."

No one on the Federated team interrupted the CFO, and needless to say the $150 million was not approved. Within three months, Goel was gone; within six, most of the top ten officers of Fingerhut had left. A year later, Fingerhut and its network of e-commerce businesses were bankrupt and sold.

"Even twenty years later you can probably hear the pain in my voice," Goel says. "It was difficult to explain what we were seeing, and it was just too difficult for them to see it. I am still haunted by the possibility of what we could have built."

Hipo Coaching Checklist – Chapter 4

Be a Master of Big Ideas and Execution

☐ **1. Make Your Big Ideas Better**
- Review your best ideas and decide which ones you want to pursue.
- Talk with others who have unique perspectives to help you shape the ideas.
- Determine how to convert them into specific actions so they can be executed in a way that delivers results.

☐ **2. How to Assess Your Good Ideas**
- There's value in applying the concept of a minimum viable product that you can test, rejigger, and retest. Some ideas can go through several iterations in a matter of weeks.
- You don't need a full business plan before you present your idea, but you do need crystal-clear thinking about how and why it will work and make a positive impact on the business.
- Consider whether the idea can be scaled up, brought to market properly, and deliver financial results.
- **For new products,** be sure you can answer questions such as these, about:
  - **Users:** Who is the user? How will it change the user's end-to-end experience, digital or non-digital? Will it substitute an existing experience? Will customers find it compelling? Will it require a change in the customer's habit?
  - **Platform:** Can the idea be converted into a platform? What will it take to do so?
  - **Scaling:** What will it take to scale up fast? What capabilities and resources will be required, and how can you get them?
  - **Competition:** What competition can you expect, and how would you deal with it? Will your idea provoke a response

(continued)

(continued)

from a giant like Amazon, Netflix, or Google? Could a small born-digital player suddenly displace you?

- **Funding:** What funding are you going to need? When will it show a positive return on investment? How much capital is needed? And what are the risks?
- **Barriers:** What will prevent you from succeeding? What bottlenecks and barriers might you encounter, and how could you deal with them?

- **For non-product ideas**, be sure you can answer questions such as these about:
  - **Vision:** What would your idea actually look like if it were to become reality? Be sure you have a crystal-clear vision of the idea and how it impacts all stakeholders.
  - **Building Blocks:** What are the five or six building blocks you would need to have in place to make that idea a reality? For example, would it require new technical or marketing capabilities? How would you build or acquire them?
  - **Financial Impact:** How will this idea make money? How long will it take to build enough scale to reduce any per-unit cost involved? How long will the added expense of high salaries be a drain on cash and profits? Where will the cash come from, and how will other parts of the business be affected?
  - **External Factors:** What changes in the external environment would make this idea succeed better? What would make it fail? Consider changes caused by governments, regulators, exchange rates, taxes, etc.
  - **Barriers:** What are the most critical hurdles you would have to overcome to bring this idea to fruition?
  - **Timing:** Is this the right time? To be sure you're not too early or too late, talk with people. Can they see the need? Do they support you? Watch your biases; you may not want to hear the negatives, but seeking out and understanding the challenges can help you overcome them.
- Don't be afraid to toss out the bad ideas. Better ones will come.

- ☐ **3. Executing Big Ideas**
  - How well you can execute your ideas depends on how well you manage people, strategy, and operations. You have to be involved in all three. On large-scale initiatives, it's important to look at every new idea through all three lenses—as well as their interconnections.
  - Think about the timeline. Questions to ask yourself include: What has to happen, by when? How fast does that have to

happen, and does something else have to happen first? Is it important to have a critical mass in place at once, or is it something to be gradually developed?

- Then assign specific goals, and follow through to make sure the work gets done and results materialize.

☐ **4. Execution Basics**

- **Show up.** Be visible, present, and mentally engaged with the people whose efforts you oversee and coordinate.
- **Set clear goals and priorities.** Crystallize the five or six things that really matter, not just for yourself, as discussed in Chapter 2, but for those who report to you. Clarity about who is doing what, by when sets the stage for accountability.
- **Stage the work.** After making the assignments, establish some milestones so you'll be able to measure progress along the way instead of waiting for the full goal to be complete. What has to be accomplished by when for each stage?
- **Stay informed.** Be aware of what's really going on.
  - You have to stay in touch to know what they're actually doing, and drive accountability through your own behavior and actions.
  - Frequent check-ins help keep things moving forward. Consider weekly meetings, or a biweekly check-in with phone calls and personal visits in between. When the stakes are high and speed is paramount, daily contact may be best.
  - Ask hard questions. Search below the surface to get to the root of why progress is slowing. Has the person lost energy or interest? Why?
  - Reward people's candor and honesty when they share bad news so potential problems aren't suppressed.
- **Address delays or problems immediately.** Work with your team to resolve them. If solutions don't emerge, devise a plan to generate some.
- **Follow through and follow up.** Actions speak louder than words.
  - Reward the doers (the ones who overcome the problems and deliver results) with praise, support, and promotions and financial rewards when appropriate. This will energize the entire team.
  - If someone fails to deliver repeatedly, face the issue head-on. Start with a one-on-one conversation; don't sugarcoat the feedback. If the person doesn't improve, you might have to put someone else in the job. Allowing non-performers to slide drains everybody's energy and puts your own job at risk.

(continued)

(*continued*)

☐ **5. Ask Incisive Questions**
  - Asking the right questions is key to gauging other people's performance and unearthing problems in execution.
  - You learn this by watching others who are good at it.
  - In any review or meeting, make note of the questions that are asked, not the answers.
  - The best questions are brief, and cut through the clutter to a pivotal assumption or bigger point. The tone is respectful, not insulting or fear-inducing.
  - Good questions create order out of complex or confusing information.
  - Create a thoughtful set of questions that you consistently ask your team. If your line of questioning is consistent, people will start to anticipate what you are likely to ask and may take actions to address the problems ahead of time.

Additional Resources

Bossidy, Larry, and Ram Charan. *Execution: The Discipline of Getting Things Done*. New York: Crown Publishing Group, 2009.

Harvard Business Review. "HBR's 10 Must Reads on Innovation," 2013.

Marquardt, Michael J. *Leading with Questions: How Leaders Find the Right Solutions by Knowing What to Ask*. San Francisco, CA: John Wiley & Sons, Inc., 2014.

5

Get to Know Customers, Competitors, and the Macro Environment

You may be so busy dealing with the immediacies of your job and the many demands on your time and attention from others in the company that you lose sight of the world beyond your four walls. Increase the return on your time and use the freed up mental space to expand your horizon. Learning about customers and competitors may already be part of your job, but every leader benefits from deepening that knowledge. A more common shortfall is in understanding the macro environment. This is the realm of geopolitics, the global financial system, social and demographic trends, and government regulation, each of which can challenge corporate leaders and can combine with deadly force.

Sorting through the onslaught of daily headlines and research reports and sifting out the nuggets is an acquired skill that is ever-more important for business leaders. As a hipo, you may have a natural bent to search for new ideas and information. If you maintain an external orientation and turn your casual scanning into a discipline, you'll be better prepared to see where the opportunities lie and what might upend your business.

Observe the End-to-End Consumer Experience

In the Internet age, power has passed to the consumer. Today some 33 percent of households are on Amazon Prime, and most people click on Amazon first before shopping elsewhere. When U.S. consumers are buying a car, about half of them click on AutoNation first. People use search engines, social media, and apps to research products and compare prices, the point being that the consumer has easy and cheap access to information, and shopping habits are changing fast.

You're not just buying a product, you're engaging in an end-to-end experience that includes everything from the time the idea of buying a product or service is stimulated in your mind by an advertisement or word of mouth to the actual purchase, use, and servicing. All of this combines to create an integral experience. Yet companies are organized in silos, and some aspects of the experience are provided by other players in the logistics chain. Even the Amazon experience depends heavily on its delivery partners.

An easy place to start to understand all the components of the consumer experience is to look at yourself as a consumer. Think of something you buy, and dissect the many parts of that buying process. What were the touch points, from first becoming aware of the product, brand, or company, to learning more about it, seeing it, using it, and buying it again? Airlines have as many as sixty-eight touch points, including the reservation process, baggage check-in, in-flight care, greetings at the destination, and dissemination of information via the website or mobile apps. Did you form an impression based on billboards and magazine ads long before you had a need? At what point did you become more interested in the product, or get turned off?

What were the moments of truth or critical decision points? Seeing something on the shelf and actually purchasing it is clearly a moment of truth. Using it is another one.

Now apply that precise thinking to your company, regardless of whether you're selling consumer products and services or items that are sold to other businesses. You should be able to see that in any position you are in, you're part of that end-to-end experience. If you're a mid-level leader, you might have the kind of direct interactions with consumers that will help you develop your instincts about how to improve their experience, but people often lose touch as they move into bigger jobs. Bosses who are more attuned to numbers than to customers don't help, as their reviews likely focus on financial results and give issues concerning customers short shrift.

At the end of the day, the consumer pays the bills. You may be keen on tapping the vast potential of the digital world, but any ideas you have for growth must be predicated on deep knowledge of what the consumer wants and needs. Despite the value of big data and analytics, you should cultivate an intuitive feel for the consumer, in part by direct observation. India's Kishore Biyani practices this regularly, even as he heads the highly successful Mumbai-based Future Group he founded. Among the company's holdings are Pantaloons, a department store chain, and Big Bazaar, the country's leading hypermarket chain, sometimes compared with Walmart. Biyani uses plenty of analysis to decide which markets and categories to compete in, but he also visits the stores twice a week. "We watch people. What are they putting in their shopping baskets, who is making the purchase decision, what are they wearing, how are they behaving," he explained. "We must be in touch with what's happening around us in society and have an understanding of what influences that."

Biyani's team prepares detailed reports that explore why people behave as they do, whether they might change, and how well they would accept something new, but there is always a human observation behind the analysis. In late 2013, Biyani noticed that girls in some local villages were going to temple in jeans, which had always been taboo. He saw that shift as a sign of two things: a greater receptivity to Western clothing and more respect for girls. "Society is shifting, and the family is allowing it," he noted, so perhaps girls and young people in general would now be more involved in purchase decisions.[i] Such observations can have enormous business implications.

Know the Competition

You may already be focused on how to differentiate your company and increase the distance between you and the most relevant competitor. Be sure you are looking at that differentiation through the eyes of the consumer. Many people consider differentiation from the inside out, as in "we're much bigger than competitor x" or "my cost is lower." Such differences won't get you sustainable sales, or higher prices, or increased market share unless the consumer recognizes and values the distinction. You also have to look beyond the differentiation you have today to what it will be next year, and two or three years out, depending on your industry.

In today's world, a lot of information about competitors is publicly available. You can listen in on investor calls, search the Internet, and pick up clues through your networks, conferences, and industry associations. Your professional peers might know which companies are giving better raises and therefore attracting top talent. Local newspapers usually report on new hires at companies in their area, and you can learn their backgrounds. It could be noteworthy, for example, for anyone in the business of making mobile devices or delivering health care that Apple has been adding health care experts to its payroll.

You may be exposed to a lot of this information already, so it may just be a matter of adjusting your attitude to pay closer

---

[i] Ram Charan, *The Attacker's Advantage* (New York: Public Affairs, 2015), and personal interviews.

attention to it. Customers will tell you something about competitors, such as why they are buying more from them than from you. And, of course, social media may be an early indicator of how well a company is tracking with investors or society in general; that's where VW first became aware of flaws in its auto emissions.

The ultimate competitive advantage comes from the critical people who make decisions, how they work together, and how they make decisions. So who are the key decision makers among your competitors? Are they risk takers? Are they forming new partnerships or supplier relationships? It could indicate a change of strategic direction. Do they stay at the cutting edge of technological developments and social trends or are they lagging behind? New people in those roles can mean your differentiation is about to be changed, by them.

What sets you apart is recognizing what others don't see. Are there companies no one recognizes as competitors yet? Maybe there's a start-up that could take your most profitable customers. We know that the digital world moves at high speed. For many born-digital companies, the incremental cost of sales is very low, so they can intensify price competition and take market share faster than historical norms. They may be in the early stages, but what if they hooked up with a company with complementary capabilities or access, or found a big infusion of funds? Watch for changes in industry structure when two competitors are merging. Your astute observation could open people's eyes and save your company.

Firsthand observation is as useful for understanding the competition as it is for understanding the consumer, and the two are often intertwined. That's why so many successful innovators and retailers walk the stores, as Biyani does, even as CEO. Walmart founder Sam Walton was famous for doing this throughout his life, including his time as CEO of what had become an enormous enterprise.

If you live in a major city, you may have shopped at a Uniqlo store, the bright modern retail chain that attracts a fashion-conscious clientele with its well-made casual clothes at affordable prices.

The company was relatively obscure through much of its seventy-five-year history, but launched into hypergrowth over the past fifteen years, expanding to more than eight hundred stores in Japan and about the same number in countries across the world by 2015. While outsiders praised Uniqlo's achievements, Tadashi Yanai, CEO of its parent company, Fast Retailing, was not resting. Well aware of the sweeping changes in retail, including the incredible power of algorithms and the success of players like Amazon, he set out in 2016 to take the business to the next level. "Digitization will change everything," he told me. "The retail, textile, and apparel industries—there is no longer such a distinction among them. The new industry is anyone who does a good job of addressing people's need for clothing."

He sought help to reinvent Uniqlo from a cadre of hipos—and took it upon himself to identify them. He knew people in the company well and trusted his instincts about the kinds of people he needed. He was looking for those who were mostly in their thirties and forties, who could grow into big leadership roles in the future, and who were change agents. He was also attuned to the way they think, saying, "A majority of our executives are left-brain oriented, which is more linear. I was mindful about picking those who were more right-side-of-the-brain. These people are very good at capturing the holistic picture. They're intuitive. The right side has more to do with photographers, designers, artists. They can discern what is beautiful and what is not." He distinguished one type from another in conversation. "If I'm having a dialogue and working with these people, I can instantaneously X-ray them," he explained.

His screening process pointed to thirty-eight leaders from a mix of business functions and hierarchical levels. It excluded some senior people in high-leverage jobs. Although those senior executives had valuable experience and insight, Yanai felt he could tap their expertise in other ways. He was convinced that the big benefit would come by combining his own strengths with what the hipos would bring.

In March 2016, the thirty-eight hipos gathered for their first meeting, which I helped Mr. Yanai facilitate. We explained what we had in mind for them. They were to continue in their current jobs, but they were being asked to do some research and brainstorming. They formed teams of six or seven people and were given an initial task: to visit the stores—Uniqlo's, those of its competitors, and even retailers that did not directly compete. The point was to research and observe the consumer and the competition, to then share those observations with their teammates, and to report back to the larger group, which would reconvene at monthly intervals. This activity was foreign to many of them, some of whom were from R&D, finance, HR, and the supply chain. But they took the task to heart, and ventured out to make their observations.

As the group reassembled to share their findings in subsequent months, they shed light on the plight of store managers. The managers were too busy in the backroom, spending time on clerical tasks and dealing with the burdensome paperwork headquarters imposed. That left little time to actually manage the business, to pay attention to consumers, to realize that products were out of stock and needed to be reordered, to suggest ideas for promotions or price changes to squeeze out excess inventory, or to inspire their employees.

As a result of those findings, the chairman and executive vice president in charge of the stores began an initiative to cut the paperwork from headquarters in half and to give store managers more business training. The job of the so-called area managers, who oversee an average of seven stores, also was rejiggered to help the stores' managers with layout, competition, and other business issues.

Another round of inputs had to do with major competitor Zara. The observations were consistent: Uniqlo's stores were generally neat and laid out beautifully. People thought Zara stores were less neat, and prices were a bit higher. Where Zara had an edge was in replenishing merchandise. Senior leaders were already aware of the time difference: Uniqlo's cycle time was roughly twelve to sixteen weeks, while Zara's was three weeks. Research traced it back to product classifications. The bulk of Zara's products—70 out of 100 SKUs (stock keeping units)—were standardized and could be produced in small batches, so there was less delay.

Those insights led to some immediate changes, such as reducing the number of SKUs at Uniqlo, and some longer-term ones, like revamping the reordering system, actions that will directly affect the company's ability to compete. It also lay the groundwork for a clear vision of what the company can become three years out.

At the same time, the practice of observing customers and competitors changed the lens through which the hipos saw the business. Some of them had never been outside their offices, but now their awareness was raised. They also understood how their work related to the company's overall direction and had the mindset to contribute more broadly. An army of hipos is to the bigger landscape and eager to implement the agreed-upon changes. As one person remarked as the September 2016 meeting came to a close, "We're ready for the structural changes we have to make, because our minds are already conditioned to it."

You don't need an invitation from your CEO, as at Uniqlo, to glean insights about competitors or to share what you see. You can do it in meetings and in conversation with your colleagues, bosses, and the people in your internal networks. Cross-functional meetings in particular are a great opportunity to learn from others and to factor your broader view and research into joint decisions.

Dissect Ecosystems

Competition today is among ecosystems, not just among direct rivals, and every company must be part of at least one. An ecosystem is a system of partners who are joined by a common platform. They can trade among themselves, with customers, and with suppliers. The platform they hook into is governed by the platform designer, which also governs the behavior of ecosystem partners. Amazon and Alibaba each has a platform that connects consumers with all the merchandisers who sell through their sites. GE has a platform called Predix, which allows information—much of it picked up from sensors embedded in machines—to flow within and between manufacturers. Its ecosystem now includes 20,000 software developers, none of them on GE's payroll, and includes big players like Cisco and TCS as partners. So the ecosystem has an army of experts finding useful ways to analyze the data for such things as reducing downtime and improving productivity. When GE sold its appliance division to Haier in 2016, the deal included a partnership for Haier to use the Predix platform.

A simple way to explain how ecosystems, not just companies, compete and how durable their competitive advantage may be is with an example you are likely familiar with: Apple. You can download onto your Apple device content created by music producers or dozens of applications created by an army of independent app developers who hook into its software platform. Apple's ecosystem also includes participants in its mobile payment system called Apple Pay, which is so far winning against competitors based on the volume of participants. The number of retail locations in the United States accepting Apple Pay in 2016 was close to two million, a huge jump from its launch in 2014. *Fortune* magazine reported in July 2016 that Apple Pay accounted for three-fourths of U.S. mobile pay transactions. Any other digital payment system must not just function well but also collect a critical mass of retail participants for the service to be appealing to consumers.

Previous generations of leaders tried to control the value chain, from suppliers to the consumer, but the new game requires new attitudes. For example, you have to accept that your ecosystem could include competitors and that it is dynamic. If you're in a small company being pulled into a big ecosystem, don't think of it as losing control. It may help you become bigger. As autonomous vehicles began to shift the landscape for automakers and their suppliers, Delphi didn't want to be left in the cold. Much of the exciting development work was happening in companies outside the traditional auto industry, at companies like Tesla, Mobile Eye, and even Google, and then the automakers kicked up their in-house development efforts. Leaders at Delphi wondered how the technology they were developing would fit in. In August 2016, they forged a partnership with Mobile Eye, giving Delphi a place in a larger ecosystem.

Monsanto's Climate Corporation is aiming to be the go-to agricultural platform, and it welcomes third-party developers to build applications for its software infrastructure. Anyone who improves the ability to guide agricultural equipment based on sensing soil composition, weather conditions, and the like will have instant access to Climate's customers. Who can join that ecosystem? Monsanto CEO Hugh Grant put it simply when speaking to investors at an event in August 2016: "The best apps win."

See Your Business from the Outside In

This is something top leaders can struggle with. Many came up within one company or industry and in a world of slower, more incremental change. The conventional logic was to focus on how your company was different from competitors and build on those core strengths. That type of career history can cause people to see the world from the inside out, as if their company were at the center of the world. The company can appear to be pretty healthy by traditional measures, but a gradual slide in sales can suddenly become a deep and permanent decline caused by a threat that wasn't even noticed because it was outside the traditional industry.

Even young leaders of digital-born companies can miss external changes, but astute leaders anticipate them. That allows time to react defensively and, more to the point, take advantage of emerging trends to go on the offense—or a combination of both. Netflix founder Reed Hastings saw that the shift to streaming technology was unstoppable. He navigated that bend in the road by switching his business model just in time from one based on sending DVDs in the mail to one based on video streaming.

Now the competitive landscape for entertainment companies is on the brink of another seismic shift. 5G is coming to mobile airwaves, promising leaps in speed for watching videos without annoying interruptions. As streaming has become a serious alternative to broadcast, players like Hulu and Amazon have been upping their game. How will companies compete when mobile streaming is a way of life?

Anticipating change and finding opportunities in it begins with the discipline of scanning the environment broadly and spotting the unstoppable trends and change makers. You can cultivate this outside-in perspective by expanding your lens to take in information on a wide range of topics, as well as globally. You may at first feel overwhelmed by the onslaught of information, but if you're truly a hipo, you will soon learn to cut through the complexity to the things that really matter.

If you work for a public company, a simple way to step outside your four walls and into the shoes of a stock analyst or shareholder activist is by listening in on analyst calls, reading analyst reports, or talking to the investor relations department about how the company is being perceived. In some cases, shareholder activists publish detailed reports about what they think management should do. Their ideas, which are often based on deep research and analysis using publicly available information, can be eye-opening to management, prompting a kind of "Why didn't we do that sooner?" response from open-minded CEOs, CFOs, and board members. Suddenly opportunities to streamline the portfolio of a business, or to trim back sales and general administrative costs to be more in line with industry averages, come into focus.

While hostile relationships between activists and managements steal the headlines, it's increasingly the case that CEOs and the board have an open ear, because the activists' outside-in perspective points to things insiders simply miss. GE CEO Jeff Immelt had had an ongoing dialogue with Trian Partners, which in October 2015 wrote a detailed eighty-page report on how GE could improve results.

Long before such relationships were fashionable, Home Depot Lead Director Bonnie Hill and the head of the board's audit committee met with the leaders of Relational Investors, an activist shareholder, to be sure the board fully understood their concerns. Long accustomed to being out of her comfort zone, in that first discussion Hill spontaneously asked, "If we were to invite you to have a representative on our board, who would you recommend?" She brought the suggestion back to the full board, and after some due diligence, they invited Relational's David Batchelder to sit on the board, where he was, in Hill's words, "an excellent board member."

Scanning the environment as a routine, being receptive to different perspectives, and searching for what is new and different will help you spot opportunities or bends in the road. Who was the first to make a business out of sharing an apartment or a car? The big successes make headlines in the *Wall Street Journal* and *Fortune* magazine, but they often start out small.

Keep your antennae up for *who* is driving change on a massive scale and bring these to your company's attention. I call such people catalysts. They could be business leaders, scientists, or people in politics or NGOs (non-governmental organizations). Ralph Nader affected the entire auto industry when he published his book *Unsafe at Any Speed*, lambasting manufacturers for lax safety standards. His advocacy reset consumer expectations and captured the attention of government regulators. It also created big opportunities for new market segments. TRW, for example, became a major supplier of air bags.

As mayor of New York, Michael Bloomberg was a catalyst when he launched a campaign against large servings of sugary soft drinks. He triggered similar actions elsewhere, causing Mexico to impose a stiff tax on sugary carbonated beverages in 2014.

Keep Up with Technology

Technology innovation lies at the heart of the world's rising standard of living. It is people who innovate, or who pick up on others' ideas and commercialize them, perhaps by reinventing a business model to get the new thing into the market. So every time there is a technological advancement, you should ruminate on it. Who will ride the entrepreneurial wave and build a big business out of it, and what are the implications for other kinds of companies?

The recent decade or so is one of tremendous gains in the areas of algorithms, sensors, sophisticated software, and ever-higher-speed computers. These things in combination are now driving changes in how we approach the sciences, from metallurgy and astronomy to life science. For example, biotech companies are now doing intensive data crunching to help with their drug development efforts. Amgen's decoding of a massive DNA sample allowed Amgen to detect a specific DNA defect that lowers the chance of having a heart attack by 35 percent. That finding set them to work on a drug that can copy the effect. Sean Harper, executive vice president of research and development at Amgen, said it could cut eighteen months off the typical fourteen-year process of bringing a drug from the lab to market.[ii]

You don't have to be technologist, but you should develop a routine to stay informed about what new relevant technologies are emerging and how they are changing the competitive landscape, bearing in mind that one new development can accelerate others. In September 2016, GE bought two 3D printing companies for $1.4 billion. Meanwhile, the Chinese government has indicated that it wants 3D companies to locate there, and in March 2016, China's first 3D-printed automobile hit the road.

Why are Jeff Bezos of Amazon fame, Larry Page and Eric Schmidt of Alphabet, and Elon Musk of Tesla interested in space

---

[ii] Antonio Regalado, "Amgen Finds Anti–Heart Attack Gene," *MIT Technology Review*, May 18, 2006.

travel? One theory is that it forces them to explore new kinds of algorithms, some of which are from the defense industry and some of which will be proprietary. To them, a $50 million investment is not huge, and they can recruit the best brains from NASA or elsewhere. Great algorithms process information faster and better—an advantage for any digital-based company.

Even old technologies may catch your interest. Corning had developed and essentially mothballed "Gorilla Glass," an ultra-strong annealed glass, three decades before Steve Jobs revived it. Jobs had been looking for a tougher, thinner glass for the iPhone. When he heard that Corning had developed such a product, he jumped on it.

Hipo Coaching Checklist – Chapter 5

Get to Know Customers, Competitors, and the Macro Environment

- Develop a discipline of scanning the macro environment—including the realms of geopolitics, the global financial system, social and demographic trends, and government regulation—to see where the opportunities lie and what might overturn your business.

☐ 1. Observe the End-to-End Consumer Experience
  - Consider your own experience as a consumer.
  - Think of something you buy, and dissect the many parts of that buying process:
    - What were the touch points, from first becoming aware of the product, brand, or company, to learning more about it, seeing it, using it, and buying it again?
    - Did you form an impression based on billboards and magazine ads long before you had a need?
    - At what point did you become more interested in the product, or get turned off?
    - What were the moments of truth or critical decision points?
  - Now apply that precise thinking to your own company, regardless of whether you're selling consumer products, services, or items that are sold to other businesses.

- Review all the ideas you have for growing the business through the customer's eyes.
- It's fine to use big data and analytics, but you should also cultivate an intuitive feel for the consumer, cultivated in part by direct observation.
- Observe your customers in the marketplace. Consider what they are buying, who is making the purchase decision, what other options they are considering, what they are wearing, how they are behaving, what other items or services they are purchasing.
- Looking across the entire, end-to-end customer experience, where do you see opportunities to improve, streamline, or add more value?

☐ **2. Know the Competition**

- Be sure you look at differentiation through the eyes of the customer or consumer. Even obvious differences won't get you sustainable sales, or higher prices, or increased market share unless the consumer recognizes and values the distinctions.
- Look beyond the differentiation you have today to what it will be next year and two or three years out, depending on your industry.
- Seek out the publicly available information on your competitors. Listen in on their investor calls, search the Internet, and pick up clues through your networks, conferences, and industry associations.
- Set up online news alerts to track their activity.
- Who are they hiring? Your professional peers can give clues about which companies are giving better raises and therefore attracting top talent. Local newspapers usually report on new hires at companies in their area, and you can learn their backgrounds. Knowing where they are increasing their staffing can provide hints about their future strategy.
- What do customers say about your competitors? Social media may give you some clues.
- What does the investor community say about them?
- The ultimate competitive advantage comes from the key people who make decisions, how they work together, and how they make decisions.
- Who are the key decision makers among your competitors?
- Are they risk takers?
- Are they forming new partnerships or supplier relationships? This could indicate a change of strategic direction.

(continued)

(*continued*)

- Do they stay at the cutting edge of technological developments and social trends or are they lagging behind?
- New people in key roles can mean your differentiation is about to be changed, by them.
- Are there companies that no one else recognizes as competitors yet? Technology companies are starting to erode profitable business from banks and other financial services firms. Is there a start-up that could eat your lunch?
- For many born-digital companies, the incremental cost of sales is very low, so they can intensify price competition and take market share faster than historical norms.
- They may be in the early stages, but what if they hooked up with a company with complementary capabilities or access, or received a big infusion of funds?
- Watch for changes in industry structure when two competitors are merging. Your astute observation could open people's eyes and save your company.
- Firsthand observation is as useful for understanding your competitors as it is for understanding your customers.
- Involve your team. Set up a regular practice of having everyone get out of the office and observe your customers and competitors. It will help them understand how their work is related to the company's overall direction and give them the mindset to contribute more broadly. Having an army of hipos on your team, all attuned to the bigger landscape and eager to implement the agreed-on changes, will greatly increase your ROYT.

☐ 3. Dissect Ecosystems
- Take time to understand your company's ecosystem—and those of your competitors. An ecosystem is a system of partners, joined together on a platform, such as Amazon's and Alibaba's platforms that connect consumers with all the merchandisers who sell through their sites, or GE's Predix platform, which allows information to flow within and between manufacturers.
  - Who are your ecosystem partners? Is your company positioned well in your ecosystem? What could you do to enhance your position? Do you have the right partners now? Will they continue to be the right partners in the future?
  - Who do your competitors partner with in their ecosystems? Are their ecosystems more extensive than yours? Which ecosystems have more power or stronger connections to customers?

- You can no longer control the whole value chain. Accept that your ecosystem could include competitors, and that it is dynamic and will continue to change over time.
- If you're in a small company getting pulled into a big ecosystem, don't think of it as losing control. It may help you become bigger.
- Stretch your perspectives to see the big picture of ecosystems across your industry. How have they been changing? Are there any trends you need to monitor?

☐ **4. See Your Business from the Outside In**
- Your role as a hipo is to view your business from the outside in—through the eyes of the customer, and in the context of the changing marketplace—to help the company avoid blind spots.
- Keep a watchful eye for any emerging threats, especially those from outside the traditional industry, which often go unnoticed for far too long, especially by senior leaders who tend to see the business from the inside out.
- Anticipating these threats will give your company time to react defensively or, better yet, to take advantage of emerging trends to go on the offense, or a combination of both.
- Set aside at least thirty minutes each week to scan the environment broadly and notice the unstoppable trends and change makers. Expand your lens to take in information from a global perspective and on a wide range of topics.
- A good way to do this if you work for a public company is to take the perspective of a stock analyst or shareholder activist. Listen in on analyst calls, read analyst reports, or talk to the investor relations department about how the company is being perceived.
- Read shareholder activists' reports. They are often based on deep research and analysis using publicly available information and frequently contain clear opinions about what management should do. Their ideas can be eye-opening and help you identify company blind spots.
- Pay attention to people in the news who are driving change on a massive scale. These catalysts could be business leaders, scientists, or people in politics or NGOs, and they often have the ability to impact industries in dramatic ways. How would they view your company? How could they influence regulation or customer views? How can you protect your company from the potential risks or take advantage of the potential opportunities?

(continued)

(*continued*)

☐   **5. Keep Up with Technology**
- Every time there is a technology advancement, ruminate on it and involve your team.
- You don't have to be technologists, but you need to develop a routine to stay informed about what new relevant technologies are emerging and how they are changing the competitive landscape.
- Consider:
  - Who will ride the entrepreneurial wave and build a big business out of it?
  - What are the implications for other kinds of companies?
  - What are the leading companies doing about it? You learn this by watching others who are good at it.
  - Remember that one new development can accelerate others. What other changes are likely to emerge?
  - Could older technologies be used in new ways in the new business environment?

Additional Resources

Charan, Ram. *The Attacker's Advantage: Turning Uncertainty into Breakthrough Opportunities*. New York: PublicAffairs, 2015.

Charan, Ram. *Global Tilt: Leading Your Business Through the Great Economic Power Shift*. New York: Crown Publishing Group, 2013.

Charan, Ram. *What the Customer Wants You to Know: How Everybody Needs to Think Differently About Sales*. New York: Penguin Group Inc., 2007.

Lafley, A.G., and Ram Charan. *The Game-Changer: How You Can Drive Revenue and Profit Growth with Innovation*. New York: Crown Publishing Group, 2008.

6

Build Your Mental Capacity

We all know that mental capacity can grow in a nanosecond if there's a will, discipline, and practice. This phenomenon is reflected in comments like "Wow, that really opened my eyes!" or "Suddenly it dawned on me. . . ." It might be a question or comment someone makes that causes you to see things differently or have a breakthrough thought. You don't have to—and shouldn't—leave this kind of thing to chance. With practice, you can build your mental capacity, just as athletes build their physical capacity. Practicing the following skills will set the stage for leaps in your thinking, judgment, and imagination.

Widen Your Lens

The more broadly you see the world, the bigger your vision is likely to be. A wide lens helps you define the opportunity and fires up the imagination. Aaron Levie was twenty years old when he and some friends from high school decided to build Box, a company that would help users share files and collaborate via the cloud. They solicited seed money from famed investor Mark Cuban by cold-calling him by e-mail, and, to their surprise, Cuban funded them. They left college to keep working on their product, moving first to Berkeley then to Palo Alto, where they obtained some more venture capital and scaled up from seven people to around twenty-five. By 2016, Box had some $400 million in sales, but to Levie, that was truly just the start. He could see the pieces coming together to create a $40 billion market for the kind of service his company provides. "We think there is a tremendous amount of upside," Levie told *Fortune* magazine in March that year.

The ability to see the big picture is a common trait among successful entrepreneurs but is equally useful in existing businesses. Top leaders are looking for those who have this ability. I saw this in a young executive, Lin Hou, at CreditEase, a financial services company based in Beijing, in a meeting in late summer 2016. The company began its life in 2006 providing microfinancing to students, entrepreneurs, and farmers through person-to-person loans. The money came from middle- and high-income individuals. In 2011, the company expanded into wealth management, offering clients a range of products—things like mutual funds, private equity, or real estate funds. As head of the product development team, Hou was in charge of sourcing those products from the likes of BlackRock, UBS, Vanguard, and Goldman Sachs.

In a meeting in 2016 among CreditEase CEO Ning Tang, Hou, a handful of other executives, and me, Tang discussed his aspiration to take CreditEase further by having a very big, very strong global asset management team that would not only source investment products but also create them.

That discussion was brief, but it ignited Hou's imagination. In a follow-up conversation, it was clear that she had immediately grasped the magnitude of the opportunity. She laid out her vision of a sizable asset management business that would create products for CreditEase to sell, then took it a step further by suggesting that CreditEase could sell those products through other financial firms. What's more, she had already begun to identify the specific actions she would take, beginning immediately, to build that capability three to five years out, including the possibility of using partnerships and alliances.

Still in her thirties, Hou had been with CreditEase from the start, and the CEO already saw her as a hipo. This confirmed it. He gave her a mandate to build the business and empowered her to do it.

You can widen your lens (or bandwidth) by reading and visualizing things on your own, or by interacting with other people. In any case, diversity is key. One of the great practitioners of expanding his lens by interacting with people is Brian Grazer, the Hollywood movie producer behind such famous works as *A Beautiful Mind* and *Apollo 13* and the TV series *Empire*. He made a discipline of it from an early age. Fresh out of college, Grazer landed a low-level job at Warner Brothers and made brazen attempts to talk to people he had no business talking to, such as Lew Wasserman, who at the time Grazer approached him was among the most powerful people in Hollywood. In his book *A Curious Mind*, Grazer describes his habit of reaching out to people from many different walks of life—athletes, fashion designers, theoretical physicists, you name it—simply to have what he calls a "curiosity conversation." Grazer's creative output speaks for itself.

Keep Learning

All of your forward momentum depends on the things you learn and how well you learn them. You're familiar with the "Peter Principle"—people rise to the level of their incompetence. That's because they stop learning. Have the humility to realize that there is always something more to know, and that many other people know more than you do. The fastest growing hipos I've known are always seeking lessons from those around them. Ask anyone who's made his way from nowhere to a leadership job he loves and he's almost certain to recall the names of many people he learned from along the way.

For Ivan Seidenberg, former CEO of Verizon, that includes the person who supervised him at his job operating a freight elevator and mopping floors while he took college classes at night. He had worked at that job for eight months before his boss mentioned to him that some companies paid for their employees to go to college. When Seidenberg asked why the boss had waited so long to say something, the supervisor said, "I had to watch you. I think you passed the test." Seidenberg made a pivotal job change after that conversation, and the lesson that someone is always watching you stuck with him, all the way to the executive suite.

Imagine you were put in charge of building an airport, something you had never done before. How, and how fast, would you learn? Kiran Kumar Grandhi faced that challenge as a thirty-something leader at GMR Group based in Bengaluru, India. Although GMR had built power plants and done highway construction, building airports was an entirely new kind of infrastructure project, so Grandhi had no one at the company to guide him. "We had no understanding of this sector," Grandhi told me, as he proceeded to explain how he went about building his expertise.

Grandhi jumped into it with both feet, because there was no time for testing the waters. The government was asking for bids to construct a new twenty-million-passenger airport at Hyderabad, and it seemed the perfect opportunity for GMR to jump onto a new growth trajectory. India's economy was opening up and would need to build the infrastructure to support it, so the Hyderabad airport was likely one of many more to come. One problem: the deadline was imminent, and GMR didn't even meet the criteria that qualified them to submit a bid. They persuaded Malaysia Airports Holdings Berhad, a publicly traded company, to partner with them for a 10 percent financial stake, and that allowed them to proceed. Malaysia Airports operated thirty-nine airports in its namesake country, so with that partnership came some expertise, and Grandhi made the most of it. He spent a lot of time building the relationships and talking with people there, picking their brains about every aspect of the business. When GMR won the bid, Grandhi had to learn much more—and fast. "What I personally did is kept an open mind and learned from as many people as I could," he said. "Whether I was meeting with an architect who was presenting a specific design, or an engineer, a consultant, or a contractor, I asked a lot of questions. Also, we had to do a lot of hiring, so I conducted many of the interviews myself. It gave me the chance to talk with top professionals from places like Singapore Airport or Hong Kong or Dubai. I was always listening for what principles they followed and for what would or would not work in India."

Grandhi attended some of the important conferences and did a lot of reading and studying reports. He also visited some thirty-five airports around the world. "I spent real quality time in those airports," Grandhi says, "learning from the operations people and top-level executives at those sites." He also turned his weekly staff meetings into learning events by devoting part of the time to discussing how other airport companies were dealing with retailers, fueling, or cargo.

Learning came naturally to him, because he'd seen his father, the founder of GMR, do it his whole life. "Whenever he meets someone, he takes an interest in what that other person is doing," Grandhi said. "He learned by interacting with people, whether it was a junior employee or a senior manager or someone in the government."

Learning and execution went hand in hand, and the airport at Hyderabad was a success. Then came a successful bid to rebuild the airport at Delhi and, after that, to build airports in Istanbul and then the Maldives. GMR Airports is today the world's fourth largest private company in the sector. "I believe that the ability to learn about new areas is the real differentiating factor for us," Grandhi concluded.

Think of learning broadly, so you're not just accumulating factual information but also deriving insights and meaning from it. Learn about your business, about yourself—your behaviors, how your mind works, what you're good at—and about other people. That means taking in lots of information—and also reflecting on it. That's when it will take you to a different place.

Build Diverse Networks

Hipos keep extending their networks and don't hesitate to reach out to so-called big shots, as Grandhi did when he needed to learn about the airport business. He did the same thing when GMR needed funding and the banks in India weren't lending. The banks had lent heavily to the infrastructure sector to build power generation plants, and those companies had a problem making payments for reasons beyond their control. The Indian government, which controls the supply of coal and gas, was in a tangle, and the power plants couldn't get enough fuel. Many of their plants were running at a third of their capacity. Grandhi ventured outside India to contact some of the most prominent people at the largest sovereign wealth funds in the world and was able to obtain funding from the Kuwait Investment Authority.

Networking is nothing more than building human relationships. Lots of them. There are many ways to do so, inside and outside your company, and many ways you'll benefit from them. Levie told me about several pivotal moments for Box, and he noted that at each juncture the networks he had developed early on were crucial to his decision making. One was around what the core business model was going to be: Should they build their product for consumers, or for big enterprise customers like Procter & Gamble and GE? Levie networked voraciously, talking to dozens of people outside the company, many of them highly experienced in the technology world, to gain a sense of the opportunity and challenges either way. It's what informed the discussion with his fellow founders and ultimately guided the choice to take the enterprise path, because, he said, "we felt there was a much bigger opportunity, and we could be far more disruptive."

Another such moment came several years later, when another company offered to buy Box for a large sum of money. This was a decision "of the greatest magnitude" and one Levie felt singularly responsible for. He told me, "It was a very, very attractive offer, something that would've been very meaningful for early employees and early investors and certainly for the founding team. So it was a real struggle to think about what to do. We knew we weren't likely to get another offer like that for two or three years, and that we would have to execute flawlessly to return to that value. But it got us thinking about our ultimate motivations and why we started the company in the first place.

"It was a tough choice, and we were without data in many ways," he explained. "We knew what the future would be if we sold, but we couldn't know what the future would be if we took the independent path. We had zero visibility."

"We had always been very mission oriented," he continued. "From the start we wanted to build a longstanding business that changed the way software works. Would we be able to accomplish that if we had a parent organization? Would our culture change, and would we be able to out-execute the competition?"

Levie reached out to half a dozen former CEOs he had built relationships with and, through that network, reached out to even more, some of whom had sold their businesses and others who had kept them. "It was really interesting to hear from them," he said. "About half of the people who had sold the company said it was the worst thing that ever happened. But other people said they sold at the exact right moment and it was the best decision they'd made. It was great to be able to have a network of people to reach out to and ask what they had gone through."

Levie took the comments to heart as he reflected on which situation was most like his. He ultimately concluded that staying independent was the way to go. "In software and technology," he explained, "your outcomes are often wildly underestimated in the successful scenario. Through a traditional lens, you tend to focus only on the likelihood of success and overlook the total potential upside. As a company, our riskiest decisions have produced the greatest upside."

Keep in mind that networks are becoming increasingly important to everyday work as companies foster collaboration among various departments, partners, and individuals in the so-called gig economy. Work groups and teams vary with the task at hand. If your talents have been recognized, you may already be participating in projects that involve more than one department or business function, as well as external partners. In fact, it's typical for hipos to be stretched thin because they're sought after. My advice is to continue those relationships by staying in touch with people long after the project is disbanded, and by all means build their trust. Trust is essential to network building.

You should also feel free to reach out to people in other parts of your company, if only to learn what they do and how they see the business. Love Goel's meteoric impact on Fingerhut (described in Chapter 4) was based on his grasp of the business's capabilities, made possible by his insatiable interest in and interaction with people in many parts of the company.

Seek Information from Everywhere

Information stimulates learning. Diversity of information stimulates creativity. Reading, conversations, and learning events are great sources of information, so be sure to include regular infusions of them in your day, week, and month.

Reading. This is one of the most important elements of my day. I'm not alone; many CEOs and directors I encounter are voracious readers. Being aware of the geo-political, economic, and technological changes in the world is essential to recognizing trends, making sound decisions, and even to allocating time properly. Investing a half hour a day in reading, seven days a week, 365 days a year, is a habit that will bring more value to you and your leadership strength than any other investment of your time. It doesn't have to be books, and if it is, don't brag about how many you've read. Just search for the new ideas, new insights, and new pieces of information.

Ideally, you want a specific time devoted to reading every day, whether it's morning, evening, or in between—whatever works for you—and make it a rule to spend a half-hour minimum. Use the time to keep up with the trends and topics that are making the headlines, as well as the ones that relate to you and your runway. Dig deeper on whatever interests you, but keep your lens broad enough to include things that do not seem directly relevant to your work. Those may be the very things that spark a great insight sometime later.

Pay particular attention to what's happening in companies or industries that are ahead of the pack, and to technologies that could be game changers in your field. When reading books and publications such as the *Financial Times*, *The New York Times*, *The Wall Street Journal*, and *The Economist*, look for the unexpected. What are the anomalies, the things that break the pattern?

Setting up the news alerts that Google and many publications offer can help ensure that you are aware of all the top stories related to your company, competitors, marketplace, and industry. Expanding your knowledge base not only helps you advance your career path, but it also gives you more information and insights to share with others, which builds your reputation as a valued "go-to person" in your network.

During your designated half hour, you probably won't have time to read everything that you find interesting. That's fine. Bookmark, print, or clip the things you want to read later and pull them out whenever you have a moment—in a taxi, on a plane, while waiting on hold for a call.

My technique is to read the "Lex" column in the *Financial Times* every day. It contains pithy commentaries by the editors on five items. Having read it for more than thirty years, I have found it to be very factually reliable and very insightful. There may be days and weeks in which I don't pick up any new trend or break from a pattern, but when I do, I reflect on what it might mean and for whom. How will competitors be affected? What are the implications for other industries? Is this a game changer? The special reports that appear every few weeks in the *Economist* also make great reading. Here the expert journalists provide great research on a wide range of topics, using a variety of sources worldwide.

Conversations. Take time to arrange conversations that expand your mental potential. These can be as simple as inviting the R&D guy out to lunch, or as in-depth as orchestrating a formal mentor relationship. It may be easier to talk regularly with friends and close colleagues, but the most valuable conversations are often the ones with people you don't know well, or perhaps haven't even met yet.

Short, targeted conversations with a wide range of individuals gives breadth to your knowledge. Having one conversation every week or two with someone outside your regular circle—yet related to your future destination—will keep your focus fresh and your energy high. Think of four or five people who might have interesting knowledge, insights, or personal connections that would help you learn more about your next landing strip. With this list, your first month or two of conversations is already planned. If you don't know these people yet, how could you meet them or who could introduce you? The next step is to write the e-mails or make the phone calls to put something on the calendar.

Before the conversations, think of what you want to contribute. What information, ideas, or personal connections would be of interest to the person you'll be talking with? Be prepared to add as much value as you receive, and the person will be eager to take your calls in the future. Also have a list of three or four key questions that you'd most like to ask this person. Thinking through these in advance not only helps focus your conversation, but also sharpens your thinking as you consolidate your own ideas on the topics.

For deeper knowledge, you may want to structure longer-term conversations that go into more depth. Monthly "mastermind" calls or industry group meetings that bring together people with similar interests can build your knowledge base and also expand your network. Explore trade associations, special interest groups, and online forums to see what's available. You can't overload your schedule—or your mind—with new ideas, so prioritization is essential. Pick the one you think will be most valuable. If the first one you select doesn't hit the mark for your learning goals, try another.

As CEO of GE, Jack Welch made a habit of asking "What's new?" of everyone he met. Many years ago I was in an elevator with him when he shot that question at me. I had recently been to a manufacturing company that was using a cutting-edge practice to reduce the dependence on working capital, so I offered a terse reply: "Zero working capital." It piqued his interest, the conversation began, and he was soon paying that company a visit to learn what they were doing. I've used a variation of the "what's new" question myself. It's surprising how much information you can pick up.

Learning Events. Attend a conference. Take a class from a leading business school—it's easy and free through Coursera or other massive open online courses (MOOCs). YouTube has hundreds of video lectures by leading CEOs, faculty, and industry experts. The world's top business schools and universities post downloadable podcasts and webcasts that you can listen to while you travel or commute. And to prove that learning events can be fast, efficient, and fun, TED Talks present five- to twenty-minute mini-lectures by leading thinkers from the fields of technology, entertainment, and design—three of the fast-moving fields that help shape how our culture evolves. TED Talks jumped from two million online views when they launched in 2006 to more than one billion collective views by 2012—and their popularity is changing the way that many conferences and other learning events are delivering their ideas. Attending a learning event in person can bring you in contact with some of the most innovative business thinkers in the world. When Kiran Kumar Grandhi was seeking the next big growth trajectory for his company, GMR, he started traveling to other parts of the world building his relationships network, and he started attending TED-sponsored conferences. "It is very global, and it really opens your mind," he said.

Stay Mentally Flexible

As you feed on information, try to become aware of how you process it. Habits of thinking can limit you or open new lanes of creativity and make you more adaptable to change. Here are things to watch for and practice to increase your mental flexibility. Keep these mental skills in mind as you work with other people. You can learn a lot by observing individuals who excel at one of them.

Reframing. Looking at things from a completely different perspective can increase your range of options and provide insight into how to overcome problems. It can help unclog psychological blockages and lead to breakthrough ideas. It will help you understand customers better and negotiate better, and it's no exaggeration to say it could even save the company, when, for instance, top leaders are able to recognize how an emerging competitor could disrupt its path.

Ivan Seidenberg led Verizon from what started as a highly regulated regional phone company that was number nine among its peers to the number one telecom network company. In his decade as CEO, he navigated a maze of government regulation, sea changes in technology, and intense competitive skirmishes from wireless and cable companies. His high potential was recognized early in his career in part because of his ability to reframe the relationship with government regulators.

Seidenberg had started his career at what was then New York Telephone as a line splicer, then joined a team to work with engineers from Bell Labs to improve the reliability of the system, and after completed his undergraduate degree, applied for and received a job as a liaison with regulators in Washington, D.C.

There was inherent tension between the phone company and the regulators. The FCC wanted minimal standards so it was easier for companies to compete; presumably consumers would benefit. The phone company wanted standards to be as strict as possible. It was Seidenberg's job to sell the latter point of view to FCC staffers, but he couldn't help but see things from the regulators' perspective as well. "Most leaders go to Washington to get what they want from the government," he told me. "I tried to change that. I went there to help the government see all the facts and facets of the industry, to help them make the industry better and make it easier for them to do their job as regulators. It requires reframing the issues and a broader view of the public and private parties."

Seidenberg's bosses didn't always accept his reframing, and it created some heat. He recalls an instance when he was leading the committee charged with figuring out how revenues should be divided among local and long distance carriers following the breakup of AT&T. The government had forced AT&T to divest its local phone services, creating seven regional phone companies. Before the divestitures, AT&T collected all the revenues and decided what to do with them. Now it was unclear how they should be divided when AT&T, MCI, Sprint, and others completed their calls through the local operating companies.

Seidenberg, now a vice president, prepared a presentation for the CEO and other top leaders, and it was a gutsy one. He argued that the plan they were pushing for—Plan A—was not the right one. "I explained that if the regulators accepted the tariff, that would mean they accepted our pricing and our cost allocations," Seidenberg said. "But I knew that the regulators had a dim view of the industry, and chances were that they'd reject the plan. If they rejected Plan A, we'd have nothing. So I recommended that we come up with a Plan B that represented some sort of compromise." Seidenberg's peers thought he had ended his career, but the CEO said to look into it further, and the committee eventually crafted a second option that the FCC accepted.

Seidenberg's natural ability to reframe the issues was one indication of his high potential, and people were watching. Fred

Salerno, who later became a vice chair of Verizon, had heard about Seidenberg from people in Washington even before he met him. The New York Congressional delegation told him, "You've got somebody special down here named Ivan Seidenberg." Bud Staley, who was president of New York Telephone, told Seidenberg to be sure to see him if he got job offers elsewhere. And when I was consulting with Staley, I happened to sit in on a presentation Seidenberg was making at company headquarters in White Plains, New York. I was so impressed by the young man's ability to clearly see opposing points of view and think creatively to solve problems, I told Staley, "This is someone you should keep your eye on."

Seidenberg used reframing later in explaining the virtues of merging with another piece of the old Bell system. "If you propose that you can save a bunch of money, that sets people in the government into orbit," he said. "We had to think hard about how the public would benefit, and we reframed the argument around attracting capital so we could invest in our assets and modernize our facilities. It's not about hiring the smartest lobbyist to defeat the government. It's actually figuring out collaborative ways to think about serving the public, which is a surrogate for our customers."

Reframing is often the key to broadening your range of options and resolving conflicts. Take care not to subconsciously eliminate some of those options before they're fully aired. This happened at a financial services company when the chief talent officer was presenting options to the executive team for introducing a new digital employee engagement survey that would periodically capture and analyze feedback. He laid out two options to begin: buy an existing software product off the shelf and get it going quickly, or spend a couple of years to create a customized system that takes into account the firm's specific needs. One of the leaders added, "Why not option three—do option two in six months instead of two years?" Everyone agreed that option three would be ideal, but it would require a heavy investment and a big commitment from management to make it a priority, things that were beyond the

CTO's control. From the vantage point of a top executive, however, it was doable, provided the rest of the team was willing to buy in and push it. The team did in fact commit the money, time, and attention, and the new software was implemented in the shortened time frame.

Asking questions is a good way to prompt other people to reframe. One example comes from a company that was losing market share, despite the fact that it had world-class technology and a cost advantage over competitors. When the sales manager met with a friend and mentor, he described how his team kept losing sales despite having offered sizable discounts. The usual tactics just weren't working anymore. The friend asked two simple questions: "What are you doing besides lowering the price?" and "Are you happy with what your suppliers are offering you?"

That's all it took. The sales manager instantly recognized that suppliers did nothing more than negotiate on price, and that they made no effort to understand the company's needs. He and his colleagues found it frustrating. As a vendor, they were doing the same thing with their customers. That conversation spurred him to reorient the sales team to an entirely new approach to selling, one aimed at helping to solve their customers' business problems.

Band height. When I teach, I try to involve people by asking a lot of questions, and it's always interesting to see the altitude of their thinking. Some people are in the weeds, debating specifics and, even with me prompting them, have a hard time lifting their view to see a bigger picture. Others immediately resort to broad, high-level statements and have trouble moving to the specifics.

As a hipo, you may love the realm of big ideas. That's how Elon Musk saw opportunity in space travel, far beyond electric cars. But to connect vision and execution, you have to be able to make a sharp descent, as Musk did in considering what would make space travel accessible. He dissected the mechanics and economics of launching spacecraft and homed in on the capsule. What if it could be reused? The cost could be cut in half.

I saw a young Chinese procurement officer make a quick descent in a session in which the chairman was explaining procurement's role in the company's new growth strategy. The company raised livestock and saw the chance to grab a huge portion of the expanding but fragmented domestic market. Profitability could be vastly improved by sourcing feed products globally, from places as far afield as Africa. It was a tall order for this young man, who spoke only Chinese, had no experience in global sourcing, and had never traveled outside the country. But he was a hipo who immediately grasped not only where the company was going but the specifics of what he would have to do to help get it there. He started rattling off what it would mean: navigating all kinds of new geopolitical and military risks and acquiring new tools for managing things like changes in currencies; he would need a foreign exchange manager, a currency trader, and an adviser on geopolitics. He was undeterred by the added complexity of his job.

Qualitative logic. Every number is a fact, but two people can see the same set of numbers and come to different conclusions about what they signify. The interpretations are qualitative, and some will be more predictive or more precisely diagnostic than others. You need only look at the performance of stock pickers to know that that's true.

Today artificial intelligence does a lot of the brainwork and promises to do much more. That will save you a lot of effort. Still, human judgment will not disappear. Despite concerted efforts to mechanize performance ratings and the like, your judgments will be especially tested when it comes to people.

Strive to make your thinking and judgments more precise. You should know when you are stepping off the terra firma of hard facts. Pay attention to the assumptions you are making, and to your risk profile. Your ability to make judgments may influence the design of the algorithms the computer uses. It may be your logic that the algorithm tries to replicate, or your assumptions that are incorporated, or your understanding of which factors make the answer more reliable that becomes a crucial input.

Hipo Coaching Checklist – Chapter 6

Build Your Mental Capacity

☐ **1. Widen Your Lens**
  - Expand your perspective to see the big picture by reading and visualizing things on your own or by interacting with other people.
  - Diversity is key to widening your lens:
    - Talk with people from many different walks of life—simply to have what Brian Grazer calls a "curiosity conversation."
    - Read a diverse range of publications.
    - Gather insights from multiple sources—online, conferences, classes.
    - Network with people from other fields, industries, countries, and backgrounds.

☐ **2. Keep Learning**
  - All of your forward momentum depends on the things you learn and how well you learn them.
  - Seek out people who know more than you do, and see what you can learn from them.
  - Don't hesitate to reach out to so-called big shots—even prominent, high-ranking people can be open to helping someone who is truly interested in learning from them.
  - When you move into a new role or take on new responsibilities, it's especially important to spend time talking with people who understand the area, picking their brains about every aspect of the business.
  - Ask lots of questions, and take time to formulate good ones. The quality of your questions will determine the quality of what you learn.
  - Turn your weekly staff meetings into learning events by devoting part of the time to discussing new insights, trends, or market events that are impacting your business.
  - Learning is more than just accumulating factual information— you also need to reflect on that information and understand what it means to you, your business, and your industry.

(continued)

(*continued*)

- Reflect on your business, yourself—your behaviors, how your mind works, what you're good at—and other people. Look for patterns, trends, changes, potential challenges, and growth opportunities.
- Consider what you can learn from each of these things, and how you can apply that learning.

☐ **3. Build Diverse Networks**

- Networking is simply building human relationships. Build lots of them, both inside and outside your company.
- Focus on building trust and adding value to the other person. Share your insights and ideas. Do you have a resource that could help? Offer introductions to other people in your network who share similar interests or goals.
- Reach out to at least one new person each week. Stay connected to the ones who stretch your thinking or spark new insights.
  - Stay in touch with people from your former jobs or people you meet during ad hoc project work in your company.
  - Reach out to people in other parts of your company to learn what they do and how they see the business.
  - Build time into your calendar, or set reminders, to ensure you don't neglect the people in your network. Decide how often you'd like to stay in touch with each person, and take responsibility for making it happen.

☐ **4. Seek Information from Everywhere**

- Information stimulates learning. Diversity of information stimulates creativity.
- Reading, conversations, and learning events are great sources of information, so be sure to include regular infusions of them in your day, week, and month.

Reading

- Set a specific time for reading every day—whatever works best for you—and make it a rule to spend a half hour minimum, seven days a week, 365 days a year. This is among the most valuable uses of your time.
- Keep up with trends and topics that are making the headlines, as well as the ones that relate to you and your runway.
- Dig deeper on whatever interests you, but keep your lens broad enough to include things that do not seem directly relevant to your work.

- Pay particular attention to what's happening in companies or industries that are ahead of the pack, and to technologies that could be game changers in your field.
- Look for the unexpected. What are the anomalies, the things that break the pattern?
- When you pick up any new trend or break from a pattern, reflect on what it might mean and for whom. How will competitors be affected? What are the implications for other industries? Is this a game changer?
- Set up news alerts through Google or online publications looking to field top stories related to your company, competitors, marketplace, and industry.
- Share your new information and insights with others to build your reputation as a valued "go-to person" in your network.
- Bookmark, print, or clip the things you want to read later and pull them out whenever you have a moment—in a taxi, on a plane, while waiting on hold for a call.

Conversations

- Take time to set up short, targeted conversations with a wide range of individuals.
- Try asking everyone you meet, "What's new?" and see what you learn.
- Have one conversation every week or two with someone outside your regular circle—yet related to your future destination—to keep your focus fresh and your energy high.
- Think of four or five people who might have interesting knowledge, insights, or personal connections that would help you learn more about your next landing strip.
- If you don't know these people yet, how could you meet them or who could introduce you? The next step is to create the e-mails or schedule the calls.
- Before the conversations, think of what you want to contribute. What information, ideas, or personal connections would be of interest to the person you'll be talking with? Be prepared to add as much value as you receive and the person will be eager to talk to you in the future.
- Also have a list of three or four key questions that you'd most like to ask this person. This will help focus your conversation and sharpen your thinking as you consolidate your own ideas on the topics.
- For deeper knowledge, consider structuring a series of conversations that go into more depth. Monthly or quarterly

(continued)

(continued)

check-in calls allow you to dig in and can also build lasting friendships.

- Monthly "mastermind" calls or industry group meetings, where you connect with people with similar interests, not only build your knowledge base but also expand your network in areas in which you want to grow.
- Explore trade associations, special interest groups, and online forums to see what's available. You can't attend them all, so pick what you think will be most valuable. If the first one you select doesn't hit the mark for you, try another.

Learning Events

- Attend a conference.
- Take a class from a leading business school—it's easy and free through Coursera or other massive open online courses (MOOCs).
- YouTube has hundreds of video lectures by leading CEOs, faculty, and industry experts.
- The world's top business schools and universities post downloadable podcasts and sitecasts that you can listen to while you travel or commute.
- To get a wide variety of new ideas in a way that's fast, efficient, and fun, listen to TED Talks. These free online video clips contain five- to twenty-minute mini-lectures by leading thinkers from the fields of technology, entertainment, and design—three of the fast-moving fields that help shape how our culture evolves.

☐ **5. Stay Mentally Flexible**
- Regularly practice these three skills to increase your mental flexibility:

1. Reframing

- Reframing is a way of viewing and experiencing events, ideas, concepts, and emotions to find more positive or collaborative alternatives.
- When you look at things from a completely different perspective, you increase your range of options and gather important insights into how to overcome problems.
- Shifting your viewpoint can help teams get "unstuck" and lead to breakthrough ideas.
- Asking questions is a good way to prompt other people to reframe.

- Review the Nano Tool article, "Shifting Mindsets: Questions That Lead to Results," from the Additional Resources section for specific ideas on how to reframe your own thinking, or your team's.

2. Band height

- What is the altitude of your thinking? Do you tend to be in the weeds, debating specifics, and have a hard time lifting your view to see a bigger picture? Or do you tend to speak in terms of broad, high-level statements and have trouble moving to the specifics?
- As a hipo, you may love the realm of big ideas, but it's essential to connect the big picture vision with the ground-floor execution.
- Practice shifting back and forth as you ponder a new issue or trend, moving from a high-level strategic view to a practical operational view.
- By expanding your band height—the ability to shift your thinking from high-level strategy to the specifics of how to make it happen—you enhance your own mental abilities as well as your value to your company.

3. Qualitative logic

- Strive to make your thinking and judgments more precise.
- Know when you are stepping off the terra firma of hard facts and into the realm of conjecture.
- Pay attention to what assumptions you are making, and make a clear distinction between the facts and your assumptions when you communicate with others.
- When you make a qualitative judgment, reflect later on how good it was and what might have improved it.

Additional Resources

Casciaro, Tiziana, Francesca Gino, and Maryam Kouchaki. "Learn to Love Networking." *Harvard Business Review* (blog). May 2016. https://hbr.org/2016/05/learn-to-love-networking.

Clark, Dorie. "Start Networking with People Outside Your Industry." *Harvard Business Review* (blog). October 20, 2016. https://hbr.org/2016/10/start-networking-with-people-outside-your-industry.

Davey, Liane. "Everyone's Network Should Provide Two Things." *Harvard Business Review* (blog). September 30, 2016. https://hbr.org/2016/09/everyones-network-should-provide-two-things.

"Shifting Mindsets: Questions That Lead to Results." *Nano Tools for Leaders* series, Wharton Executive Education, The Wharton School (University of Pennsylvania). August 2012. http://executiveeducation.wharton.upenn.edu/thought-leadership/wharton-at-work/2012/08/shifting-mindsets.

PART II

TAKING CHARGE OF YOUR GROWTH AND CHOOSING YOUR NEXT BIG CAREER MOVE

7

How, When, and Why to Make a Leap

You may or may not aspire to become an entrepreneur, but thinking like one as you plan your career will give you a huge advantage in today's environment. It's been common for hipos to move upward by assuming greater responsibility within their vertical silos. But your brain can deal with a bigger, broader picture, so you should seek experiences that will build on that innate talent.

You can expand your range of capabilities and deepen your knowledge and judgment faster by putting yourself in new and increasingly complex and ambiguous situations. It's wise to seek support from other managers and your company's HR department, but decide for yourself what your next challenge ought to be. The trend toward open labor markets, where employees can easily apply for any opportunity at the company, puts opportunities for leaps that are exponential well within your reach. You'll benefit more from each move if you know what you need to develop next, how to maximize the learning in each new situation, and how to build the support you need.

Remember the flip side of increasing workplace transparency: your reputation will follow you. You can't swoop through a series of jobs that look good on a résumé with no concern for what you've left behind. Pay attention to what you are learning and *how* you are taking charge of each new situation and accomplishing your goals. Let your drive and ambition—even your impatience—propel you, but focus on the substance of your leadership, not your political connections and maneuverings.

The Virtue of Leaps

Venturing into unknown, ambiguous new situations versus doing an expanded version of the same job is the best preparation for the challenges you'll face at the highest organizational levels, when you suddenly have to integrate many functional areas, balance conflicting interests, and sort through a large number of variables. Most successful leaders will describe such challenging and pivotal growth experiences along their path. Some companies build them into their leadership development plans, but in many of the cases I've seen, the person sought them out, even when it meant leaving his or her comfort zone or the company. "I've always taken on things that are challenging and will have a big impact on the company," Tony Palmer, president of global brands and innovation at Kimberly-Clark, said when I asked him about his growth path.

Set your clock back some forty years and imagine you are a well-educated city person dropped off in a remote village in northern India in the middle of the night. Why? Because you aspire to be a top leader in a global consumer company, and your employer is testing you. You have a place to sleep and a family to eat with, but little else. Your survival kit consists of first aid, bedding, a mosquito net, and a flashlight. Communication and transportation systems are, of course, far less developed than they are today. Your bosses say they will visit you a few times over the next two or three months, but you are basically on your own, charged with devising and piloting a project to improve villagers' lives, something that can be scaled up across India.

That's the experience Vindi Banga had as a management trainee at Hindustan Unilever. He was shocked when he woke up the next day to find that the villagers took care of their personal hygiene in public. "It was like being on Mars," Banga told me. He had to get comfortable living as the villagers did, and at the same time, to complete the assignment, he had to quickly gather the information he needed to identify the problem he would try to fix. "I spent hours talking with the local people about the village, their families, their work, and their aspirations and concerns," he recalls. "I had to win their trust to do what I was sent to do."

He was struck by how unhealthy the lack of covered drainage was. It created pools of water where insects bred. From his engineering background, he knew that simple drainage pits would address the problem, but his ideas were not exactly welcome. "The locals said it had always been like that, so it wasn't a great concern," Banga noted.

He finally persuaded the village headman to experiment and see how it might help. Banga, the headman, and another villager dug three drainage pits, circular holes roughly ten feet deep and six inches across, around the village well. They filled each pit with small pieces of brick and gravel to prevent it from filling up with silt and sand.

The experiment worked. Overnight the area around the well was transformed, and word quickly spread. A village meeting followed, where Banga showed a site plan for additional wells, and the villagers undertook the work as Banga supervised.

When Banga's boss arrived weeks later, he was duly impressed with the results. Banga got a nice promotion, and others followed as he continued to expand his leadership capabilities. He ultimately became CEO and chairman of Hindustan Unilever (he has since retired). "I got the lessons of a lifetime," he said, recalling his village experience. "I learned to listen to people, to understand their needs and win their support. And I gained confidence in myself, in my ability to quickly size up a new situation and to overcome the hurdles." [i]

---

[i] Bill Conaty and Ram Charan, *The Talent Masters: Why Smart Leaders Put People Before Numbers* (New York: Crown Publishing Group, 2010), and personal interviews.

Every hipo must make leaps repeatedly. Here's a crucial one you will likely need to make somewhere in your development: let's say you're a sales manager and you have a chance to go to a larger company and be a profit-and-loss manager—in charge of the profitability of an entire product line, for example. The job is totally different in content, scope, visibility, and pressure. It requires an entirely different skill set, a new cognitive architecture or mindset, and networks beyond your former discipline. You'll need to work horizontally across functional silos like manufacturing, marketing, and product development and assign a set of goals with sales targets as a subset. You'll have to make tradeoffs of different kinds factoring in a wider range of variables and select and motivate people for non-sales jobs. If you figure out how to do all that, you've made an important leap for anyone hoping to be a high-level business leader.

Compare that with another move: you're a sales manager in one territory, and now you get three territories to manage. The job is bigger, but it's essentially more of the same. The growth is linear.

A similar job in another country can be a leap, because you have to build new networks, understand a different regulatory and political system, and master differences in the competitive landscape, culture, and practical things like distribution networks. I knew Mike DeDomenico when he was a rising leader at Praxair, succeeding as an industrial sales manager in the United States. To further test and develop him, he was put in charge of distribution in Canada. After succeeding in the new country and a different part of the business for roughly three years, he was put in charge of distribution in Europe, where he then faced the much greater complexity of multiple countries.

Geographic leaps are fairly typical for the most promising leaders in large global corporations. CEO A.G. Lafley and head of HR Dick Antoine made a global assignment a requirement for the highest offices at P&G. Deb Henretta, one of the people identified as having the potential to get there, was moved from a marketing role in P&G's laundry business to head the fading global baby care business. That in itself was a leap, from a functional job to a global one. She reinvigorated baby care, and after five years, Lafley and Antoine thought she was ripe for an assignment in another country. She loved her job running global baby care and her family was happily settled in Cincinnati, so she didn't immediately warm up to the idea. But when a leadership job in Singapore opened up, she saw the opportunity for tremendous growth, and she and her family accepted it.

In the United States, Henretta was in charge of one product category. In Singapore, she ended up running all categories for fifteen Asian countries. She had to understand each country's culture, politics, and marketplace, establish the competitive advantages in each, and allocate resources across countries and categories. Not only that, but she had to deal with frequent crises, whether a tsunami, an earthquake, or a terrorist attack. Five years into the job, she said people often commented on her ability to stay calm in a crisis. She attributed it to the maturity she gained in a place full of unexpected challenges. She also learned to accept fast change. Recalling her visits to Vietnam, she said, "When I first started going five years ago, the streets were crowded, but they were crowded with bicycles and scooters, and if you saw an occasional truck on the street it was an unusual sight. And now in places like Ho Chi Minh City, it's largely cars and trucks on the road. . . . Maybe I should have been embracing change more in my previous job, but you certainly can't *not* do it here."[ii]

Moving from one department or functional silo to another is a leap many hipos make early in their careers. It forces you to see things from a different perspective and creates a fuller picture of how the organization works. A move outside your area of expertise can be particularly unnerving if your confidence is built on being the most knowledgeable person in the room. A leader with

---

[ii] Ibid, , pp. 140–41, and personal interviews.

little background in medicine or technology, for example, can feel overwhelmed when suddenly put in charge of world-class experts. Jeff Immelt handled it; GE Medical Systems was one of his stops on the way to becoming CEO of GE. It's common at GE to rotate leaders among its diverse businesses. Jim McNerney, the former CEO of 3M, then Boeing, is a GE alum who had leadership jobs in GE Capital and in GE's appliances and aircraft engine businesses. You can't succeed in those jobs unless you can quickly grasp the fundamentals of the business and gauge talent in the new area.

Taking a job in which you are leading highly respected people who are much older and more experienced than you is also a leap. Pat Gallagher, chairman and CEO of Arthur J. Gallagher & Co., a Chicago-based risk management and insurance brokerage company, described how he made this rite of passage. When he joined the business fresh out of college, his father and uncle were running it, and they immediately sent him out to make cold calls. He had served as an intern and observed his dad and uncle for years, so he was prepared, and he had a knack for it. "Going out and asking people if they'll let you work on their insurance was natural to me," he told me. "I loved it from the beginning."

The young salesman quickly became one of the company's top producers, and his dad and uncle wanted him to take over a sales unit. "Here I was just twenty-six years old—and I looked a lot younger than that—with people significantly older than me reporting to me. That experience taught me how to lead from behind in a sense. When you've got a forty-year-old reporting to a twenty-six-year-old, you're not telling the person what to do. It's a matter of leveraging expertise. My approach was to say where I thought I could be helpful. I told people to let me know when they needed me to bring in resources to help close the sale. I respected their age and their seniority and we ended up working together very well."

Aaron Greenblatt, the thirty-two-year-old CEO of G&W Laboratories, a pharmaceutical company based in South Plainfield,

New Jersey, describes the leap he made when he was put in charge of the supply chain at the age of twenty-five: "Suddenly I was leading teams of people whom a very short while ago I would have knocked down their doors to get their advice."

Making Leaps Without Leaving Your Company

You'll know when it's time to make a leap. Your learning curve will flatten. You'll crave new learning, new challenges. You'll be bored and anxious to make a greater impact. At the same time, you'll be doing the job in less time and getting great feedback from others who are telling you that you're doing an excellent job. The key here is hunger for a new challenge, yet excellent performance in what you're doing. Trying to jump the wire without succeeding in your current job first is nothing more than blind ambition.

If you're on a hipo list or have the kind of boss who stretches you, the next opportunity may come to you. More often, you will have to find ways to extend your runway by advocating for jobs or tasks that will challenge you. Seek them out and demonstrate your readiness in meetings, where your bosses, peers, and subordinates see how you think and lead. If you conduct yourself well, other people may put in a word to support you or talk about you in positive ways. In those situations, humility matters. Demonstrate your best qualities and let people infer what more you can do.

You don't necessarily have to take on an entirely new job or a job at a much higher level. Jobs at a similar level but in a different part of the business can be huge learning opportunities. Employers who know that you fully understand the product and the industry may be more inclined to move you from finance to marketing, say, or from Latin America to Asia.

A lot of work is project based, so your best growth may be on an ad hoc team that arises around a new initiative or to resolve a key challenge. These opportunities often involve cross-business-unit issues that don't fall in anyone's current domain. Fight for them.

They will give you a chance to exercise your skills in seeing and integrating diverse perspectives.

Don't play it safe by choosing projects where you can expect sure success. Instead, seek the ones that involve complexity or ambiguity. Your potential grows by taking on the "wicked problems" that stretch your thinking, demand ingenuity, and literally force you to shift your perspective.

Even without a task force or team, you can take it upon yourself to solve the organization's biggest problems. Your fresh view on the situation might actually lead to a breakthrough. As CEO of GE, Jack Welch put Jeff Immelt in charge of air compressors precisely because he knew nothing about them; the theory was that because Immelt carried no baggage, he would objectively sort through the seemingly intractable problems in that business. Welch was right. Immelt did and later became Welch's successor.

You can get ideas about what these intractable problems are by reading the CEO's messages and other corporate communications, or by asking around. In this age of openness, there's little to stop you from seeking information and solutions and finding people who will be receptive to your ideas. Be sure to focus on the substance of the issues and your sincere desire to learn and accomplish something. Self-promotion won't fly.

As you search for opportunities, look for a good boss or mentor. Your immediate boss can be your best ally or biggest roadblock in making a leap. Even kind and supportive bosses can hold you back if they become too reliant on your current skills and don't want to let you go. Life is too short to work for someone who restricts your potential. Instead, find the talent magnets, the bosses with a reputation for advancing their direct reports. You may already know these people. If not, do some networking to find out who they are. They're out there.

In his article "Secrets of the Superbosses," published in *Harvard Business Review* in January–Febraury 2016, Sydney Finkelstein tried to explain a pattern he had observed, writing: "If you look at the top people in a given industry, you'll often find that as many as half of them once worked for the same well-known leader." One reason Finkelstein gave was that the superbosses gave their protégés chances to dramatically compress their learning and growth: "Chase Coleman, a disciple of Julian Robertson, says that his former boss 'was good at providing a steep learning curve for people who excelled at their first task.' In fact, just three years after Coleman joined Tiger Management as a technology analyst, Robertson sent him off with $25 million to start his own fund. Larry Ellison took a similar approach, says Gary Bloom, a former executive VP of Oracle who later became CEO of Veritas. 'One thing Oracle was incredibly good at was on a continual basis throwing new responsibility at people,' Bloom notes."

You may be able to make a leap by taking on volunteer work. A board position in a local nonprofit, for example, could expand your strategic leadership skills. The reference book *Global Leadership: The Next Generation*, by Marshall Goldsmith and colleagues, lists scores of ways to expand your skill sets in the areas most needed by current and future global leaders and may lay the foundation for a leap.

Take heart in knowing that top leaders are seeking talent and that data bases are being constructed that will whittle down the bureaucracy and opacity around job promotions and leadership development. You'll have more opportunities to be noticed, and individual bosses will have less control over your fate. Politicking and loyalty will give way to the substance of leadership.

Build Your Own Support System

I've talked to many successful leaders who say how lucky they were to have had a mentor who helped them immensely. Whether the relationship is by luck or by design (my belief is that outstanding talent does not go unnoticed for long), great mentors can accelerate a leader's growth. There's no need to wait for recognition;

you can and should actively pursue people who can help you grow. Decide what mentoring you need based on a precise definition of what you need to build.

That's what Aaron Greenblatt did as a very young man, and he credits it with helping him stay focused on his purpose in life and business. (See Chapter 8 for more on Greenblatt's sense of purpose.) G&W Laboratories was started in 1919 by his great-grandfather. His father, Ronald, was the third-generation CEO whom Aaron says was his first mentor. "My father was my spiritual mentor," Greenblatt says. "Starting when I was four or five and continuing into my teens, he helped me clarify what was important to me, and avoid things that would be a waste of time. It all centered around realizing my potential, in whatever endeavor I embarked on. He used to tell me that if I was going to sweep the warehouse floor I should do it to perfection.

"Then when I was twenty-one Gary Newell came into my life," Greenblatt continues. "I had become an independent business owner through Amway and got involved in their mentorship program. Gary is a former NFL football player who had worked at Johnson & Johnson for a while and founded an international youth ministry called Outreach America. He was pretty high up in Amway and part of the mentorship program. I was in pharmacy school at the time, but I already knew I wanted to join the family business, and Gary was a great role model. For four or five years I would drive to North Carolina or some other distant destination every week for meetings, because I knew the mentorship program would be more valuable to me than my formal education. Gary gave me emotional support, encouraged me, and opened my eyes to the world of leadership and team building. Those were the passions that I ended up relying on when I entered the business world."

As Greenblatt entered the family business at a difficult time for the company, then grew into increasingly bigger jobs, he continued to seek advice from people he could learn from. His first act as CEO was to build an advisory board of business luminaries as a support system to guide and encourage him for the challenges he knew he would face as he aspired to drive his company to the next level as a thirty-year-old CEO. "You know you are going to make mistakes," he said. "I have always tried to surround myself with people who had my best interests at heart and could help me avoid some of those mistakes, and fix the ones I'm bound to make. That helps you manage your precious time and energy and helps you achieve your goals exponentially faster. Their generosity inspires me. I can never pay it back; I can only pay it forward. In accepting their help, there's a commitment and responsibility to do something with their gift, to realize my purpose that drives me."

The best mentoring is by a boss who observes you and coaches you in real time. Some cutting-edge companies are implementing systems for bosses to log feedback digitally and requesting that they discuss it with the employee with some regular frequency, such as once a week; follow-up surveys ask people to rate the usefulness of the feedback they're getting from their bosses. Until such practices become widespread, great coaching from your boss is likely hit or miss. In any case, there's nothing wrong with seeking help from people at higher levels or outside the company. Seek those who can help you build your capabilities, not just facilitate upward mobility. Don't go seeking favors or a coattail to ride.

As you reach out to experienced pros, you will likely get some backlash. You may need a sounding board to help you deal with any problems that arise among peers, customers, or bosses who feel you are going around them. Understand that such "people problems" are rooted in fear and must be handled with sensitivity.

Bonnie Hill's Multiple Leaps

"There's no way I was supposed to get to where I was," Bonnie Hill said as she began to describe her growth path to me. "I was raised in poverty in a broken family and almost dropped out of high school. Early in my marriage, when my husband had a heart attack, my only goal was to ensure that my infant daughter didn't grow up on welfare." That simple motivation launched her journey to earn a bachelor's degree, and from there, into a far-ranging series of for-profit and nonprofit experiences that continually thrust her into new and challenging situations. She earned her bachelor's, master's, and Ph.D. while working full time and became vice president and general manager of the Kaiser Center (a subsidiary of Kaiser Aluminum and Chemical), commissioner of the U.S. Postal Rate Commission, assistant secretary of the U.S. Department of Education, special advisor to George H.W. Bush for consumer affairs, Secretary of State and Consumer Services for Governor Pete Wilson, dean of the McIntire School of Commerce, and chief executive of The Times Mirror Foundation. She has served as director on numerous boards, including Home Depot, Niagara Mohawk Power, Yum!, and Hershey Foods.

"Every job I've ever taken I had no experience in," she says, "but I never hesitated to take on a challenge."

One such leap occurred at Kaiser, where she insisted on getting out of her comfort zone. She had been heading the Marcus Foster Education Institute, a nonprofit aimed at improving educational opportunities for disenfranchised children in the area of Oakland, California. There she crossed paths with a handful of high-powered executives who were on the Institute's board. When she announced she was planning to leave her position, she says: "They all started talking with me and asking me what I wanted to do. I started with what I *didn't* want. I didn't want to go into public affairs or HR. I wanted to be responsible for the bottom line." Cornell Maier, CEO of Kaiser, asked, "How's your finance?" to which she replied, "It's really rotten—but I'm a quick study." The conversations continued, and one of the executives, Tim Priest, offered Hill a position as administrative manager for planning and control and saw a chance for her to help with a public relations crisis he was facing.

The Kaiser Center had an exhibit in contemporary art that was highly controversial, and the company wanted to remove it. Priest asked Hill to take on the challenge and, in his words, "She took care of it." Months later he asked her to look at the Kaiser Center complex and give him her recommendations. "I had no idea why," Hill says. Two weeks later she was appointed vice president and general manager of the Center.

At the same time, Hill was on the board of the Chamber of Commerce, and Priest encouraged her to take a trip to Washington, D.C., with the Chamber to promote legislation that would help Oakland. It was a fateful trip. "The chairman and president of the Chamber of Commerce invited me to have dinner with them and members of President Reagan's staff," Hill explains. "And the two women we met took a liking to me and invited me to the White House the next day. I couldn't stay long enough to meet the president, but I met Press Secretary Jim Brady. He had his shirt sleeves rolled up, and was very gregarious."

That was the day Jim Brady and President Reagan were shot. Hill continued, "It was shocking. That evening I called one of the women I had met to ask how the President and Jim were doing. They apparently were impressed that I bothered to call and stayed in touch with me. About two years later, I got a call from the White House asking me to take a presidential appointment."

Torn over whether to take the post as a commissioner on the U.S. Postal Rate Commission, Hill talked with Maier and Priest, and Maier told her, "It's a rare opportunity. You need to take it. You can always come back home."

More leaps followed, to dean of the McIntire School of Commerce at the University of Virginia, and then to executive positions at Times Mirror, and to board positions, four of which faced crises during her tenure. Each time, she broadened her perspective and carried forth lessons, including those she picked up from others along the way.

"There were people in my life who helped me get past the really tough points," she says. "I was determined to get an education and outrun poverty, but there were times when other people pushed me.

When I finished my bachelor's in record time, my counselor said, 'Okay, you need to go for the next degree, because everybody has an undergraduate degree.' My advisor at Cal State, where I got my master's, insisted that I get my doctorate at UC Berkeley. He called me the last day of registration and urged me to get over there. 'They're expecting you,' he said.

"I didn't realize it was called coaching and mentoring at the time, but way back in my first corporate job, my boss, Tim Priest, took me under his wing. And I carried his advice throughout my career. He told me, for example, to always make sure I understand what's going on in a meeting, saying that a lot of people are afraid to ask questions, and that I shouldn't fall into that trap. Years later when I found myself sitting in meetings where people were using acronyms and shorthand, I would stop them and say, 'Would you mind repeating that in English?'"

Hill captures the essence of making a leap when she advises young hipos not to be limited by their particular skill set. "I will take on anything because I believe that I can learn quickly enough to do it," she says. "You have to be a quick learner, find out what it is you're dealing with, and who. Be informed, be confident that you can figure it out, and don't be afraid to ask for help. When you do that, the sky is the limit."

Leaps Outside the Company

If your HR department gave you this book, they want to keep you! Work with them as you plot your course. Sometimes, however, you have to leave the company to make a leap.

As you contemplate that choice, be sure you're separating fight from flight. That is, never give up your tenacity and make excuses for doing so. In any job, you have to put up with some guff, provided you see some real benefit in the future. Maybe you didn't get the promotion or raise you wanted. Sort out why. Some reasons may not be related to you. Maybe the company is withholding raises for the sake of internal equity. Maybe someone has a different kind of job in mind for you.

If you are no longer growing in that environment, your immediate boss is not stretching you, you've run out of opportunities to broaden your thinking and skills, and you're not succeeding at getting things changed, face it. Don't wait until the job becomes an energy drain or stay at the company only because of its marquee name. That's when it's time to seek your next opportunity somewhere else.

There's no better way of finding opportunities in the larger world than tapping into a broad network of friends and acquaintances, starting with those already in your social networks. You and your connections know at least a little about one another. As you reach out, it may be tempting to start with your strong ties and good friends, but it's important to check in with your weaker ties, too. According to research by Stanford sociologist Mark Granovetter, weak ties are, ironically, more helpful than strong ones in landing jobs. That's because your close friends have similar networks and are likely to lead you back to job opportunities you already know about, while weak ties connect you to more diverse networks and job options that you likely haven't heard of.

The digital world facilitates finding your next job in numerous ways, by posting positions that are opening up, and also by making it easy to know what companies are growing and how they treat their employees. Just in the past two years I've seen some companies begin to seek candidates from nontraditional backgrounds and without the usual pedigrees. This is a major change—and a great opportunity for hipos.

Once you've found an interesting opportunity, start a set of notes where you bring together company information and your reactions to their brand, strategy, culture, and customer focus. To find out more about companies you're not familiar with, start with corporate websites and then quickly look elsewhere for critical and independent tests of the official view. Search for articles—archived, as well as current—in financial publications such as *The Wall Street Journal*, *The New York Times*, *Forbes*, *The Financial Times*, *Fortune*, *Wired*, and *Fast Company*. Also check out industry-specific journals or trade publications.

Hoover's, a business research outfit owned by Dun & Brad-street, provides extensive company info and industry data for public companies; *The Wall Street Journal*'s Company Research gives insights on company leaders, financials, analyst ratings, and industry comparisons; Google will turn up many ways to connect, including some that are highly specific. LinkedIn can help you find contacts inside the company you already know or one of your current connections knows. Warm introductions always open doors faster than unsolicited e-mails. And if you can't find anyone through your own connections, Glassdoor.com and Vault.com can give you inside information, including surveys and employee reviews on the company, people, and culture. You may also know of other good sources for checking out companies. You don't need to gather reams of data, just enough to give you a feel for whether this company can offer you an opportunity that will align with your goals and values.

Weighing a Job Change

"How do I know if this is the right move?" That's a question almost everyone asks when facing a potential fork in their road. Whether the job opportunity came from your own search or from a head-hunter out of the blue, you should weigh the new opportunity from multiple angles. Does it help you build skills that will prepare you for the next two or three flights in your journey? Does the company have a development program? Does it lock you into a prescribed role, or allow you to make leaps? Who would your boss be, and how might that person help you?

Above all, does it hold the promise of letting you live your purpose and achieve the accomplishments and fulfillment that are important to you? Do you have a passion for this next leap in your path? If so, don't worry about your weaknesses—"I don't know how to do those calculations" or "I don't have experience in that country." Find what fits your greatest strengths and passion and affords you the chance to take them further.

Jeff Bezos has said that passion is the best criterion for weighing your opportunities. In his talk at the "re: Invent conference," blogger Zach Bulygo quotes him as saying, "Never chase the hot thing . . . you need to position yourself and wait for the wave. And the way you do that is you pick something you're passionate about. That's the number one piece of advice that I'd give to someone that wants to start a company or start a new endeavor inside of a bigger company. . . . I'd take a missionary over a mercenary any day. Mercenaries want to flip the company and get rich, missionaries want to build a great product or service—and one of those paradoxes is usually the missionaries end up making more money anyway . . . pick something you're passionate about."

Say you're in a well-established company where the compensation is excellent and you've been told you're on track for steady progress. Now you've been asked to join a start-up with lower initial pay and a fair amount of risk, but you'll have the chance to grow faster and further if the company succeeds. Your comfort level with risk is an obvious consideration. But you also have to think about which company would provide the best environment for your personal and career growth. Which job would give you challenges that excite you and stretch you in new directions? Where would you learn more that will help you fulfill your larger business and personal goals?

Avoid generalities and consider the specific context. Conventional wisdom has been that large, multilevel companies can slow the advancement of hipos, but HR practices are decidedly changing, and hipos can benefit from the excellent training many big companies provide. Some of the top CEOs today got their early training from GE, P&G, or Nestlé. For the new generation of hipos, it's Amazon, Apple, Google, Facebook, and Netflix. Learning the tricks of the trade at these companies can extend your runway and give you a great foundation for launching a start-up or taking a bigger job elsewhere. In India today, one of the top launching pads for hipos is Hindustan Unilever. It's known for being the best place to learn marketing, and it has produced, by some estimates, the largest number of marketing executives and CEOs in India.

Again, don't take a job merely for the halo effect of enhancing your personal brand; take it for the learning. But for practical reasons, you might want to avoid working for a disreputable brand or a dying company, which could make finding your next job an uphill battle. Think of the suspicion that even the most honorable executives of Enron or Arthur Andersen had to face as they interviewed for their next jobs. Although you can't always anticipate what could happen to a company's reputation in the future, do your research and trust your gut feelings when you interview with a new company. If you get just the slightest suspicion that something isn't right, then pass it by, even if the job is a big step up with a substantial pay raise. The potential damage may not be worth it.

Explore the health of the business and its culture. How well does this company adapt to change? Does it seem to recruit and place the right talent? Can it implement its strategy? And how well do people work together across functions or geographies? Watch what pronouns people use; beware if "they" and "I" are more typical than "we."

Your Exit Plan

The way you end your assignment in your current job can live on in the company's internal lore for years, even decades. The stories people tell about it will shape the opinions of every person your role touched, as well as people you have never met. Think back to the stories you heard about people who left a company you worked for. What did former colleagues focus on? Would you want to be remembered and talked about that way? Psychology's "peak-end rule" states that people have a tendency to judge an experience by how it was at its peak time (the best or worst) and how it was at the very end—rather than on the sum total or average of all the interactions. There's no way to change the peak experiences now, but you can make a major difference in the end experience. Here are a few guidelines to keep in mind as you prepare your exit plan:

- *Be respectful.* Focus on the positive reasons for the change and be honest about it.

- *Smooth the transition.* Do what you can to help the person coming in behind you.

- *Stay in contact after you leave.* The people you're leaving behind could be customers for you tomorrow.

Your Entrance Plan

As you enter a new role, nothing trumps humility. People will relax and be open with you if you go in with an attitude of curiosity and a desire to learn about the new situation. Listen more than you speak, reach out to solicit ideas and insights from others, and avoid judgments at all costs. You aren't a solo performer, so you will be judged on how well others follow your lead. And the higher you rise in an organization, the more your success will depend on the others who work with and for you. You know you're doing well when those around you are actually rooting for you to succeed. That kind of trust is built by meaning what you say and delivering on it. People will see through you if you are being devious or doing things for your own personal gain.

Creating good first impressions and early encounters will jump-start your success, as long as you follow through by maintaining your curiosity and willingness to learn. What are your most important first steps? Focus on connecting with people, listening, learning, asking questions. Hipos ask more questions than they answer. Let people know that you are seeking their input and help. Building your new networks and gathering information will help you understand the new situation and how it works—from multiple perspectives—before you start making changes. Hill recalls advice from her former boss and mentor when she was put in charge of the Kaiser Center: "He suggested I get out of my office and go meet everyone in their space. I did exactly that, and I have to say that those relationships got off on a good footing."

Here are a few other key points to keep in mind in your first days, weeks, and months:

- **Avoid saying "This is what we did in my former company."** It implies that your old way was better and will leave the impression that you are stuck in the past. Even if your old way was better, keep quiet at first. After you have learned the new landscape and built a strong network, then it's time to synthesize the best of the old and new ways of working. Create a novel approach that is all your own, and test it out with others who want to see you succeed.

- **Be very skeptical about applying what you did well in the past to the new situation.** Even more important than what you say is what you do. Your old success patterns and ways of leading and interacting served you well in your last environment, but may not work at all in your new one, especially if you've moved to a new country or culture. Rely on your perceptual ability and creativity to develop new ways to win and succeed, not just for yourself but also for the organization you inherit.

- **Sharpen your self-awareness.** Your moods have specific effects on the people around you, and these effects may be quite different in your new environment than they were in your previous one. Pay close attention to how people respond to you, verbally and non-verbally, and adapt your approach accordingly.

- **If people challenge you, focus on your shared future.** When Alan Mulally entered Ford as CEO in September of 2006, someone asked him during an early meeting, "Why should you be the CEO of Ford?" implying that he didn't know the auto business. "This is a consumer business," the challenger said. "You come from Boeing which is business-to-business." Mulally treated the question with respect, but was blunt in focusing on the future. He nodded and asked, "What condition is Ford in right now?" The people in the meeting told him that Ford was very short of cash and might go into bankruptcy. He said, "This is the team that's put the company in that position. It's my job to help you lead this company in a positive direction." He made it clear that what was ultimately important would be his role in turning Ford's leaders into a winning team.

- **Leave the past in the past.** Don't carry in any chips on your shoulder from your old job. It was a big disappointment for Mulally not to be named CEO of Boeing, but he didn't bring any residual bitterness with him as he entered Ford. He commanded respect because he had led the 777 project with great success, and he came into Ford with a fresh perspective that guided him as he stabilized its financial position. Most members of the team remained with him.

Hipo Coaching Checklist – Chapter 7

How, When, and Why to Make a Leap

- To expand your range of capabilities and deepen your knowledge and judgment faster, put yourself in new and increasingly complex and ambiguous situations.
- It's wise to seek support from other managers and your company's HR department, but decide for yourself what your next challenge ought to be.
- You'll benefit more from each move if you plan it by thinking about:
  - What you need to develop next
  - How to maximize the learning in each new situation
  - How to build the support you need
- Remember that your reputation will follow you. Pay attention to how others perceive:
  - What you are leaving behind
  - How you are taking charge of each new situation
  - The way you are accomplishing your goals
- Stay true to being the kind of leader you truly want to be.

☐ **1. When to Leap**
  - Simply put, you'll know when it's time to make a leap.
  - Your learning curve will flatten.
  - You'll crave new learnings, new challenges.
  - You'll be bored and anxious to make a greater impact.
  - At the same time, you'll be doing the job in less time and receiving great feedback from others who are telling you that you're doing an excellent job.
  - The key here is hunger for a new challenge, yet excellent performance in what you're doing.
  - Don't try to jump into a new role without succeeding in your current job. You need to tackle the current challenges first by expanding your knowledge and skills and improving your relationships and networks. Then you'll be ready to leap.

☐ **2. The Virtue of Leaps**
  - As a hipo, you'll have many opportunities to change roles. Look for opportunities that are truly leaps (tackling new, complex, or ambiguous situations that stretch you), rather than simply linear growth (doing an expanded version of the same job you've been doing).

- Leaps will:
  - Force you to venture into the unknown
  - Require an entirely different skill set, a new cognitive architecture or mindset, and broader networks beyond your former discipline
  - Bring you totally different content areas, scope, visibility, and pressures
  - Often involve integrating many functional areas, balancing conflicting interests, and sorting through a large number of variables
  - Feel like a big challenge and come with a higher level of risk
- Potential leaps you may want to consider:
  - An entirely new challenge that involves complex or ambiguous situations
  - A similar job in another country
  - A move from one department or functional silo to another, if it forces you to see things from a different perspective and gives you a fuller picture of how the organization works
  - A role in which you are leading highly respected people who are much older and more experienced than you or who have expertise you don't have
- Taking leaps (rather than opting for linear growth) is the best preparation for the challenges you'll face at the highest organizational levels.

☐ **3. Making Leaps Without Leaving Your Company**
- If you're on a hipo list or have a great boss, sometimes the next opportunity will come to you. But don't leave it to chance.
- Look for ways to extend your runway by advocating for jobs or tasks that will challenge you.
- Demonstrate your readiness in meetings, where your bosses, peers, and subordinates see how you think and lead—but be humble about it. Avoid bragging about your accomplishments. Simply demonstrate your best qualities and let people infer what more you can do.
- A lot of work is project based, so your best growth may be on an ad hoc team that arises around a new initiative or to resolve a key challenge. These opportunities often involve cross-business-unit issues that don't fall in anyone's current domain. Go for these!
- Look for volunteer opportunities that offer similar cross-business-unit interactions.

(continued)

(continued)

- Even without a task force or team, you can take it upon yourself to solve the organization's biggest problems. Your fresh view on the situation might lead to a breakthrough.
- To get ideas on what problems to tackle, read the CEO's messages and other corporate communications, or ask around.
- Continually seek information and solutions and find people who will be receptive to your ideas.
- Be sure to focus on the substance of the issues and your sincere desire to learn and accomplish something.
- As you search for new opportunities, look for a good boss or mentor with a reputation for coaching and advancing his or her direct reports. Your immediate boss can be your best ally or biggest roadblock in making a leap.

☐ **4. Build Your Own Support System**
- Actively pursue people who can help you grow. Decide what mentoring you need based on a precise definition of what skills or networks you want to build.
- The best mentoring is by a boss who observes you and coaches you in real time, offering frequent feedback.
- It's fine to seek help from people at higher levels or outside the company, but look for people who can help you build your capabilities, not just facilitate upward mobility.
- Be mindful of organizational politics if you reach upward (above your boss) for mentoring. Make sure you maintain good relationships with your boss and co-workers to avoid any fear or jealousy on their part.

☐ **5. Leaps Outside the Company**
- If your HR department gave you this book, they want to keep you! Work with them as you plot your course. Sometimes, however, you have to leave the company to make a leap.
- Separate fight from flight. No job is perfect, so you may have to be tenacious.
- Signs that it may be time to leave a company include:
  - You are no longer growing in that environment; you've run out of opportunities to broaden your thinking and skills
  - Your immediate boss is not stretching you and there are no other internal mentors available
  - You're not succeeding at getting things changed
- The best way to find external job opportunities is to tap into a broad network of friends and acquaintances, starting with those already in your social networks.
- Reach beyond your strong ties and good friends, and check in with your weaker ties, too. Weak ties are, ironically, more helpful than strong ones in landing jobs.

- Digital advances are offering a growing number of ways to find your next job, from instantly posting new positions to offering easy ways to see which companies are growing and how they treat their employees.
- Once you've found an interesting opportunity, start a set of notes that includes company information and your reactions to their brand, strategy, culture, and customer focus.
- To find out more about companies you're not familiar with, start with their corporate website and then quickly look elsewhere for critical and independent tests of the official view.
- Explore articles in the archives of the *Wall Street Journal*, *New York Times*, *Forbes*, *Financial Times*, *Fortune*, *Wired*, and *Fast Company*, as well as the Hoover's Business database.
- LinkedIn can help you find contacts inside the company you already know or one of your current connections knows. Warm introductions always open doors faster than unsolicited e-mails.
- If you can't find anyone through your own connections, Glassdoor.com and Vault.com can give you inside information, including surveys and employee reviews on the company, people, and culture.
- Follow up with any other good sources you know of for checking out companies.
- You don't need to gather reams of data, just enough to give you a feel for whether this company can offer you an opportunity that will align with your goals and values.

☐   6. Weighing a Job Change
  - As you consider new opportunities, it's important to weigh them from multiple angles:
    - Does it help you build skills that will prepare you for the next two or three flights in your journey?
    - Does the company have a development program?
    - Does it lock you into a prescribed role, or allow you to make leaps?
    - Who would your boss be, and how might that person help you?
    - Above all, does it hold the promise of letting you live your purpose and achieve the accomplishments and fulfillment that are important to you?
  - Dig deeper in your research to find insights into:
    - How healthy is the company—financially and culturally?
    - How well does this company adapt to change?
    - Does it seem to recruit and place the right talent?
    - Can it implement its strategy?
    - How well do people work together across functions or geographies?

(continued)

(*continued*)

- Watch what pronouns employees use; beware if "they" and "I" are more typical than "we."
- Remember, don't take a job merely for the halo effect of enhancing your personal brand; take it for the learning.
- Avoid working for a disreputable brand or a dying company, which could make finding your next job an uphill battle. If you get the slightest suspicion that something isn't right with a company, then pass it by. A better opportunity will come along—one that won't tarnish your reputation.
- Do you have a passion for this next leap in your path? If so, don't worry about your weaknesses or skill gaps. Your passion will inspire you to increase your skills and speed up your learning curve.
- Be informed, be confident that you can figure it out, and don't be afraid to ask for help. When you do that, the sky is the limit.

☐ **7. Your Exit Plan**

- The way you end your assignment in your current job can live on in the company's internal lore for years, even decades—and could affect your reputation for life.
- Consider how you want to be remembered after you are gone.
- Psychology's "peak-end rule" states that people have a tendency to judge an experience by how it was at its peak time (the best or worst) and how it was at the very end—rather than on the sum total or average of all the interactions. There's no way to change the peak experiences now, but you can make a major difference in the end experience.
- Keep these guidelines in mind as you prepare your exit plan:
  - *Be respectful.* Focus on the positive reasons for the change and be honest about it.
  - *Smooth the transition.* Do what you can to help the person coming in behind you.
  - *Stay in contact after you leave.* The people you're leaving behind could be customers for you tomorrow.

☐ **8. Your Entrance Plan**

- As you enter a new role, nothing trumps humility. People will relax and be open with you if you go in with an attitude of curiosity and a desire to learn about the new situation.
- Focus on connecting with people, listening, learning, asking questions. Listen more than you speak, reach out to solicit ideas and insights from others, and avoid judgments at all costs.
- Let people know that you are seeking their input and help. Building your new networks and gathering information will help you understand the new situation and how it works— from multiple perspectives—before you start making changes.

- You will be judged on how well others follow your lead. Build trust with them by listening well, acknowledging their perspectives, being transparent about your objectives, meaning what you say, and delivering on it.
- Avoid the common pitfalls people often fall into when they enter a new company:
  - Avoid saying, "This is what we did in my former company." Instead, synthesize the best ideas from your former company and your new company to create a novel approach that is all your own. Test your new approach out with people who want you to succeed.
  - Be very skeptical about applying what you did well in the past to the new situation. Instead, rely on your perceptual skills and creativity to develop new ways to win and succeed, not just for yourself but also for the organization you inherit.
  - Sharpen your self-awareness. Your personality, moods, and leadership style may have very different effects in your new environment than in your previous one. Pay close attention to how people respond to you, verbally and nonverbally, and adapt your approach accordingly.
  - If people challenge you, focus on your shared future.
  - Leave the past in the past. Don't carry any chips on your shoulder from your old job. Instead, see this as a fresh start and focus on the positive opportunities for moving ahead.

Additional Resources

Lore, Nicholas. *The Pathfinder: How to Choose or Change Your Career for a Lifetime of Satisfaction and Success*. New York: Touchstone Books, 2012.

Watkins, Michael D. *The First 90 Days: Proven Strategies for Getting Up to Speed Faster and Smarter*. Boston, MA: Harvard Business Review Press, 2013.

8

Track Your Mental Health and Work/Life Balance

For a life that's truly fulfilling, I encourage you to plan your growth trajectory from two perspectives: your business achievement and your life satisfaction. I've known too many "successful" people who achieved their business ambitions—the battles you win, the ranks you attain, the status and power you achieve, the money you make, the material goods you acquire, and the other ways you get the outside world to perceive you—but lost their health, their families, or their sense of fulfillment in life. And for people with high potential it can be just as unrewarding to focus only on living a "happy" life, one centered on personal well-being and family but with no big accomplishments to call their own.

Many people believe business achievement and life satisfaction are mutually exclusive goals, that you need to focus on one at the expense of the other. That's not true. You need to include both in your ongoing priorities, and revisit the balance between them at each new decision point along your runway. Curb the excuses and come to terms with the fact that if there's an imbalance, it's because of you. Maybe you love what you're doing so you're losing sight of other things, or you're escaping a bad marriage by logging more time at work. You also need to mind your mental health— the anxiety, stress, and disappointment that can creep in along the way and undermine the best-laid plans for success in your life.

Business Achievement

Your business achievement, by my definition, has to do with the external gains you seek. You wouldn't be a hipo if you didn't care about these things, because they form part of your motivation to excel and achieve. But take time to identify the specific goals that you want—the senior leadership position, the new house or car, better educational opportunities for your children, the chance to sit at the table with decision makers who influence the world—and ask yourself *why* you want them. Do you want power and influence for the thrill of attaining it, or to prove your importance, or to accomplish something useful and valuable to the world?

Kiran Kumar Grandhi (see also Chapter 6) was personally drawn to the infrastructure business in India "because it was a chance to contribute something big to society, to change life in the place I live. When I travel to some of our airports or highway projects, I feel proud that we were able to deal with the bureaucratic environment and get things done. It is something I personally feel strongly about, that suits my personality, and is what I'm aspiring to do."

Knowing the outcome, knowing *where* you want your increasing power to take you, will help you plan a runway that will get you there more directly. Is accumulating money your sole objective and means of keeping score, or is it a means to care for your family, expand your horizons with new experiences, or contribute to others through donations or investments? Obsession with money without a clear understanding of why you want it can lead people to sacrifice friendships, families, personal interests, and—if it has driven them to cut corners or become dishonest—conscience.

The lives of many individuals I have known over the years convince me that we derive happiness not from the trappings of success but from the satisfactions of accomplishment, which you earn by using your talents fully and knowing that you are achieving things that truly matter to yourself and others.

To clarify your achievement goals, take a moment to picture your retirement dinner. You're about to make a short speech highlighting three accomplishments that stand out above all others in your professional life. What would you say about them—why were they important to you and what did you learn from each of them? The answers will help you design your next runway.

Life Satisfaction

What you're doing now may be a calculated point in your long-run plan or a job delivered by circumstance. Either way, look at yourself closely and honestly and decide whether the work itself gives you satisfaction. It isn't enough to find a good match for your skills and strengths. You need to be sure that what you're doing (and how you're doing it) gives you intrinsic rewards. A choice that may look right to your head may be all wrong for your heart. And if your head and heart are not aligned, you won't be truly happy in the long run.

How can you test whether or not what you're doing will be ultimately satisfying? A few simple benchmarks will give you a good idea:

- **You are true to yourself.** A crucial way of assessing the fulfillment you get from your work is how well the work honors your values. Does the work that you do, day in and day out, allow you to express the parts of you that you value most? Does it allow you to be true to yourself, instead of yielding to outside pressures or the expectations of others? Bill George, whose stewardship as chairman and CEO of Medtronic earned him numerous leadership honors, went on to become a professor of management at Harvard Business School, where he has taught leadership since 2004. In his popular book, *True North*,[i] George focuses on leaders who are genuine—true to themselves and what they believe in.

---

[i] Bill George with Peter Sims, *True North: Discover Your Authentic Leadership* (San Francisco, CA: John Wiley & Sons, Inc., 2007).

He calls them "authentic" leaders. Leaders who remain true to themselves engender trust and develop honest connections with others. Because people trust them, they are able to motivate others to higher levels of performance.

George's "defining moment" came in 1988 when he was driving near his home in Minneapolis. He had left Medtronic to become an executive vice president at the much larger Honeywell. "I had turned Medtronic down for the third time in ten years to become its president, most likely because the company wasn't large enough to fit my image of what I should be doing. . . . I looked in the rear view mirror and saw a person in agony who was in the midst of a crisis and drifting away from his True North. . . . I was getting caught up in the politics and appearances at Honeywell, rather than ignoring them as I had done in the past. I was even wearing cufflinks to impress senior people, something I had never done before. In that instant I recognized that Honeywell was not the right place for me, nor was I proud of what was happening to me in this environment." As a result, he returned to his old company. "When I walked through Medtronic's front door six months later as its new president, I felt like I was coming home."

As you look at each next step along your runway, ask yourself: Will this allow me to express my genuine self and remain the kind of leader I'll be proud to be?

- **Your work means something.** Having a sense of meaning or purpose has been the top-ranked job factor for decades. Many highly successful people value it more than income, advancement opportunities, job security, or life-balance. Meaning is that inner knowledge that what you are doing matters, that you are making an important difference in the lives of individuals or the advancement of the world. Yale researcher Amy Wrzesniewski describes it as the difference between having "a job, a career, or a calling." People with a job orientation see their work as a means to an end— something that helps them pay the bills and feed their families. Those with a career orientation view work as a means to advancement—leading them to ever-higher levels of success or prestige. By contrast, she says, those with a calling orientation focus on the "enjoyment of fulfilling, socially useful work." To achieve your full potential, keep looking until you find work that is intrinsically satisfying to you—work that is so meaningful, exciting, or fulfilling that it energizes you to do it. This is a huge driver of capacity. The energy that you get from doing meaningful work increases your resilience and helps you bounce back from difficulties. It also gives you the strength to maintain long-term momentum and achieve big goals.

- **You regularly experience "flow."** Flow is a state of being completely immersed in what you are doing. Time slips away as this totally engaging state of focus kicks in, dissolving all distractions. All that remains is a merging of you and the task you are absorbed in. Athletes describe this state as being "in the zone," and it often leads to peak performance. When you're in flow, you may not feel happy in the moment—in fact, you most likely aren't thinking about your feelings, you're just totally absorbed in what you are doing. Yet Martin Seligman, the father of Positive Psychology,[ii] lists flow

---

[ii] Martin E.P. Seligman, *Authentic Happiness: Using the New Positive Psychology to Realize Your Potential for Lasting Fulfillment* (New York: Simon & Schuster, Inc., 2002).

as one of the key ingredients of "authentic happiness," the kind of happiness that leads to a flourishing, fulfilling life. Consider your work history so far. What kinds of activities in each of your past roles allowed you to slip into a state of flow? Was it mentoring others? Designing strategies? Leading teams? Collaborating with partners? Innovating? Speaking? Writing? Learning something new? Making things happen? Whatever puts you "in the zone" at work has the potential to extend your runway as a leader. As you map out your journey ahead, how can you include more of these types of experiences?

- **You regularly use your unique strengths.** Studies show that we feel most fulfilled when we are using our natural talents and strengths. Not sure about your natural aptitudes? Your past can hold clues to your present and future. What activities really engaged you as a child? What did you do when you were left entirely to your own devices? What did you excel in? Which of your mental faculties were you using? When were you happiest? If you can't remember, ask the people you grew up with— parents, siblings, close friends. The facts you learn from this inquiry can give you new ideas about what you should be doing tomorrow.

  You can get deeper insights with the StrengthsFinder 2.0, a book and an assessment tool based on Gallup's forty-year study of human strengths.[iii] It ranks you on the thirty-four most common talents expressed in the business world. Gallup's and a wide range of other research also show that the more you use and build on your unique strengths at work, the happier and more productive you are.

[iii] Tom Rath, *StrengthsFinder 2.0* (New York: Gallup Press, 2007).

- **Most of the stress in your life is positive, rather than negative.** Every human life has stress, but not all stress is negative. We experience stress whenever we grow: when we take on a new job, start a new relationship, or learn a new skill. Any kind of challenge or competition is stressful—but it can also be the source of some of the most satisfying joys in life. New research is also showing that how you think about stress makes all the difference. Stanford researcher Kelly McGonigal has found that your perceptions about stress determine how your body physiologically responds to the situation. If you believe that stress is harmful, your blood vessels dilate, your blood pressure rises, and you experience a range of other negative physiological consequences. If you believe that stress is invigorating and exciting, then your blood vessels do not dilate, and your body doesn't suffer from the negative consequences. As you think about the stress in your life, does it tend to be invigorating and exciting—or damaging and draining? Make changes to shift the balance toward the positive.

- **People enjoy being around you.** While we can sometimes fool ourselves, we can rarely fool everyone around us. People are generally attracted to others who are truly happy, so focus for a moment on the mirror of the people around you. When they interact with you, do they show that they genuinely like and respect you? Do they give you feedback that they enjoy being around you? Not necessarily verbal feedback; more like a spark of connection in their eyes. Does their body language convey something positive—either upbeat excitement or a sense of relaxed appreciation? If people don't enjoy being around you, it might be because you are focusing so intently on business achievements that you are not interested in them or neglecting your life satisfaction.

Your ongoing runway, then, should reflect the balance of business achievement and life satisfaction that works for you. Be intellectually honest about what you are willing to give up personally to achieve the business success you imagine. In solitary moments, reflect on: "Would I have done something differently in the past? What would I like to do differently in the future?"

Regularly revisiting and rebalancing your drive for achievement with what you personally value will ensure you can proudly look back on your life twenty years from now without deep regrets.

Grandhi observed, "Once you become successful, you tend to ignore your family and close friends. About five years ago I realized it had happened to me. Now I travel with the family as much as possible, or don't travel as much, and I protect family holidays and my kids' birthdays. I consciously remind myself that I have to do this to keep my life in balance."

Find a Meaningful Focus

What do you want to accomplish? Most hipos have a driving ambition to achieve or create something big. This natural tendency leads you to see beyond what's been done in the past. At your most ambitious, you dream of the ultimate, whatever it might be and however impossible it may seem at the time. When automobiles were rich men's toys, Henry Ford was determined to put them within the reach of his own factory workers. His peers thought him insane. Google founders Sergey Brin and Larry Page envisioned their start-up's destination when they were still in college: "To organize the world's information and make it accessible." Presumptuous? Maybe. Prophetic? Absolutely. No promise is too big if you can deliver on it.

The hipos who turn out to be game changers don't have to ask themselves about their focus—they already have a big idea or a driving vision. They are looking far beyond their immediate runway, and their focus never wavers as they relentlessly push through obstacles that would stymie other people. They have psyches that can see past the visible range of experience. It's why they often see customers' needs before the customers even know they have them. Steve Jobs famously aimed to create "the next great thing." Not only that, he promised that it would be "insanely great." Time and again he delivered.

Tech is a hotbed of such people, but hipos with unwavering focus are found in all types of businesses and industries. Take Ingvar Kamprad, the founder of IKEA. Kamprad started before World War II with a small mail-order business in Sweden that sold a miscellany of items from fountain pens to jewelry and furniture. As more and more of his sales came from the booming postwar market for furniture, in 1951 the twenty-five-year-old entrepreneur dropped all of his other products to focus on it. From the outset, Kamprad was obsessed with keeping costs and prices low. But IKEA was not just a budget furniture business. Kamprad's goal—stated repeatedly in speeches and company literature—was to "create a better everyday life for the many," which he executed by offering "a wide range of well-designed, functional home furnishing products at a price so low that as many people as possible will be able to afford them." For more than half a century of sustained growth around the world, those products have literally walked out of the showrooms: customers stroll through an IKEA store, taking notes on the pieces they want, and pick up the goods, packed in IKEA's famous flat packs, on the way out. Kamprad called his mission statement a "concept," but Harvard strategy professor Cynthia Montgomery prefers the word "purpose." Purpose, she says, is how "any company describes itself in the most fundamental terms possible—why it exists, what value it brings to the world, what sets it apart, and why and to whom it matters."

Many successful start-ups are built on the founder's sense of purpose, which gives the whole organization a clear focus. Chip Conley was a pioneer in the boutique hotel business, starting his San Francisco–based Joi de Vivre chain at age twenty-four during the dot.com boom. His edgy, idiosyncratic hotels became a great hit, and JDV grew to seventeen hotels and $100 million in revenues in just a few years. Then came the bust, and business fell off sharply. At one point he was considering closing the company. Wandering despondently though a bookstore looking for self-help books, he came upon Abraham Maslow's famous *Toward a Psychology of Being*, in which Maslow laid out his concept of the hierarchy of human needs.(You may remember his pyramid of needs: food and shelter at the base, good family relationships and the like in the middle, and self-actualization at the top.) Conley had read it years before, but picking it up and browsing it again, he had an "aha" moment that told him what to do with his business.

"I was reminded of why I had started the company in the first place," he told Mike Hofman of *Inc.* magazine.[iv] His original idea had been catchy, but rereading Maslow taught him that he needed to reach higher—to the top of Maslow's pyramid, where needs such as meaning and creative expression reside. "I [had] named it Joie de Vivre because I wanted to create for myself and for others a sense of the joy of life in the workplace. And I felt a real calling to the hotel industry.

"The company we ran had connected on a lot of levels with a lot of people, and if we could get back to that, I felt like we could get ourselves out of the doldrums. And we did." The new hotels, specializing in business travelers, offer such amenities as a spa-like experience and morning yoga classes. By 2011, when Conley sold most of his shares in the company, it boasted thirty-three hotels and revenues of $240 million.[v] He credits his success to maintaining an unwavering focus on bringing that sense of Joi de Vivre to

---

[iv] Mike Hofman, "The Idea That Saved My Company," *Inc.*, October 1, 2007, http://www.inc.com/magazine/20071001/the-idea-that-saved-my-company.html, accessed November 23, 2016.

[v] Andrew S. Ross, "Big money, plans for Joie de Vivre hotels," *SFGate*, June 8, 2010, http://www.sfgate.com/business/bottomline/article/Big-money-plans-for-Joie-de-Vivre-hotels-3186112.php.

the workplace. He has gone on to write several books based on the lessons he learned. In 2013, he was hired by Airbnb, the private bed & breakfast network who also believe in his vision. He also started Fest300, billed as "the definitive guide to the world's best festivals," another venture that grew out of his passions in life.

Your passion may actually be more important than you think. Research by the University of Pennsylvania's Angela Duckworth into the predictors of achievement show that grit, "the passion and perseverance for long-term goals," may be just as important—or maybe even more important—than your talent, luck, or intense desire. Grit predicts success more reliably than talent or I.Q. It foretells the amount of energy you'll invest in projects, and how quickly you'll bounce back when you encounter obstacles or setbacks. Grit, she says, is "holding steadfast to that goal. Even when you fall down. Even when you screw up. Even when progress toward that goal is halting or slow." Passion is a key ingredient of grit, which is why it's so important to tap into your underlying passion as you map your future.

Reflect for a minute on the focus of your own runway. You don't need to create "the next great thing" like Steve Jobs, but you do need a focus you can commit to—one that relates to both your values (what's important to you personally and professionally) and your runway (the ideal path that you want to travel). Keep it in the back of your mind and continuously look for ideas and opportunities that support it. It will make you excited to get up in the morning and keep you motivated and energized through the challenges that lie ahead. For years, Mahatma Gandhi endured a barrage of personal hardships in his quest to bring independence to India through nonviolent means. His unwavering commitment to the ultimate goal is what kept him going through trials that would have destroyed a leader without that drive.

If your focus is not as strong as it needs to be, you may need to revise it to make it worth committing to 100 percent. If it seems to be too strong—so that it alienates those close to you or interferes with your health and well-being—you may want to temper it by putting a little more focus on increasing satisfaction in your personal life.

A hipo's intense drive and unwavering focus often makes others uncomfortable, or even hostile. Some of the people you outdo will not be able to cope with it. That's to be expected. You can't control everyone's reactions. However, I urge you not to ruin your health or your closest relationships in search of a career goal that will ultimately bring only fleeting happiness. What matters are your skills, your grit, your resilience to live with disappointments, and your focus on your potential, your goals, and your opportunities.

Protect Your Mental Health

Most of us live with some degree of anxiety about work. We want the self-satisfaction and the rewards that come with accomplishment and we want to contribute to a larger sense of purpose. We often worry a little about how well we're doing and push ourselves for that competitive edge. Even when we accomplish a goal, we're seldom satisfied for long. Pretty soon we're raising the bar or reaching for the next big challenge.

While anxiety helps drive you, it can take a much more malevolent form, creating a sense of apprehension or fear. Gone too far it can be toxic, disrupting your natural desire to do better and distracting you from what's important. It can cause physical symptoms that include digestive problems, chest pain, dizziness, high blood pressure, disturbed sleep, loss of appetite, and serious depression.

When anxiety crosses the line, you're not the only one affected. In this connected world, anxiety is easily spread, infecting departments, divisions, and even entire companies. We've all heard stories of bosses who impose impossible demands on other people, then scream at and otherwise demean those who don't deliver. Such tactics have proven to be destructive and are easily exposed. Your bad habits and even your mood can create anxiety in others.

It's your job as a leader to create a healthy work environment and to relieve other people's anxiety when it escalates. There are plenty of reasons for it, from the uncertainty of cutbacks to the fear of failure or losing face. Just being in the wrong job can stir feelings of insecurity and anxiety, and, of course, pressures from outside the workplace factor in.

You can help other people deal with their anxiety by taking a longer view of the situation, engaging them in creating solutions to the problems at hand, and being honest about the possibilities and risks. The goal is to channel anxiety in productive ways, to convert it into inspiration and positive action.

To do any of that you must first know how to manage your own stress. Hipos are known for putting themselves in the kind of challenging situations that make most other people overly anxious. They have the confidence, the courage, and as one hipo, Aaron Greenblatt (see also Chapter 7) puts it, "the faith" to deal with it. But even hipos can suffer from too much anxiety. When things go in an unexpected direction, or the team comes for answers you don't have, it can shake your confidence and relentless optimism. Watch for symptoms in your physical condition or behavior. Are you flying off the handle? Drinking more? Sleeping less? Revisit your work/life balance and be honest about whether the job is still right for you. Seek support from your mentors, friends, and family, or professionals. If you reach the conclusion that you have to make a major change in your life, remember that the next trajectory is another chance to learn and grow and to realize your ultimate sense of purpose as a high-potential leader and a human being.

How Aaron Greenblatt Found His Focus

At thirty-two, Aaron Greenblatt is still coming into his own, although he heads G&W Laboratories, the company his great-grandfather founded. The New Jersey–based maker of generic pharmaceuticals was struggling financially and sales were one-eighth their 2016 level when Greenblatt joined some seven years earlier. He helped stabilize and expand the business, and as CEO since the age of thirty, has been envisioning and now executing on a far bigger future for the company.

Was his vision something he could realize, or just a wild idea? The answer, he says, is a matter of faith. "Faith applies to a lot of different things; whether in your spiritual life or your business life, it's a matter of believing in the unseen—believing very deeply in something before others can see it or believing that something can happen that you don't necessarily have proof of," he explains. "I have a vision, but I can't necessarily see every step along the way.

"What you can be sure of," he says, "is that it will make you uncomfortable. So you have to commit to living outside of your comfort zone."

He experienced that discomfort early on and repeatedly throughout his work life. He was still in his teens when he decided his goal was to do his best in the family business. He knew it would be useful to have a pharmacology degree, but he was terrible in science. He went to pharmacy school anyway. "It forced me to get comfortable being uncomfortable," he says.

Greenblatt graduated far from the top of the class and took a job at G&W, which was in the midst of a turnaround. "We were having financial problems, pricing problems, supply problems, and quality issues with the FDA. And my very first week our new president initiated a restructuring.

"I was put in charge of a newly created supply chain department that enveloped several other departments. Almost immediately I had to lay off some experienced people who didn't belong in the new structure, and for the next two and a half years had to plan the schedule around getting enough cash to bring in more materials and keep the business going."

From there he moved into packaging, the largest department, and then to the commercial side of the organization, none of which he had experience in. "All along the way I was leading initiatives for issues that I was tackling for the first time, while being surrounded by veterans on the topic. That was one version of being uncomfortable. But I also worked at being uncomfortable in areas that are my strength," he explained. "I looked for bigger opportunities and took on decisions where I didn't have all the knowledge and had to surround myself with people who did."

As his vision grew to the point of wanting to grow a multibillion-dollar organization, he knew being uncomfortable would be a way of life. But, he says, he has a foundation. "I know myself, what my beliefs are, and what my moral or spiritual framework is. Once you have that and you know yourself, it's a matter of crafting a life that supports that foundation, starting with the friends you choose, and the people you surround yourself with.

"My father was one of my spiritual mentors. He helped me gain clarity on who I was and what was important to me when I was very young, so I could understand my potential as a human being and choose my goals. Knowing why you're doing what you're doing is part of the foundation, part of what convinces you to commit to being outside of your comfort zone. Integrating your core values into your life allows you to live with peace, rest, joy, and gratitude. To me, that is living at peak. Discovering my passion for entrepreneurship, and then for leadership and team building, defined the direction I wanted to take and the skills I needed to build. It gave me a clear focus and turned into more of a calling and the platform for me to live my purpose and my life: helping people realize their potential."

Finding your own meaningful focus and balancing your drive for business achievement and life satisfaction is not easy. It takes time and effort and regular check-ins to ensure you are staying in tune with what is truly important to you. The reward is knowing that you are living your purpose, that you are using all of your high potential in service of what is ultimately most important to you.

Hipo Coaching Checklist – Chapter 8
Track Your Mental Health and Work/Life Balance

- For a life that's truly fulfilling, plan your growth trajectory from two perspectives—your business achievement and your life satisfaction.
- Revisit the balance between these two at each new decision point along your runway.

☐ **1. Business Achievement**
- Your business achievement, by my definition, has to do with the external gains you seek.
- Take time to identify the specific goals that you want—a senior leadership position, a new house or car, better educational opportunities for your children, a chance to sit at the table with decision makers who influence the world?
- Then, just as important, identify *why* you want them. What will each accomplishment bring you—greater happiness, peace of mind, more respect, a sense of pride?
- Knowing both *what* you want and *why* you want it will help you plan a runway that will get you there more directly.
- To clarify your achievement goals, take a moment to picture your retirement dinner. You're about to make a short speech highlighting three accomplishments that stand out above all others in your professional life. What would you say about them—why were they important to you and what did you learn from each of them? The answers will help you design your next runway.

☐ **2. Life Satisfaction**

How can you test whether or not what you're doing will be ultimately satisfying? A few simple benchmarks will give you a good idea:

- You are true to yourself.
  - Does your work honor your values?
  - Does the work that you do, day in and day out, allow you to express the parts of you that you value most?
  - Does it allow you to be true to yourself, instead of yielding to outside pressures or the expectations of others?
  - Does it allow you to be the kind of leader you'll be proud to be?
- Your work means something.
  - Do you have an inner knowing that what you are doing matters, that you are making an important difference in the lives of individuals or the advancement of the world?

- Meaningful work helps you achieve your full potential because it is so intrinsically rewarding and fulfilling that it often energizes you to do it.
- The energy that you get from meaningful work increases your resilience and helps you bounce back from difficulties. It also gives you the strength to maintain long-term momentum and achieve big goals.
- Is your runway leading you toward a life of meaning and fulfillment? If not, now is the time to change that.
- You regularly experience "flow."
  - Flow is a state of being completely immersed in what you are doing. Time slips away, distractions dissolve, and all that remains is a merging of you and the task you are absorbed in. Athletes describe this state as being "in the zone," and it often leads to peak performance.
  - Whatever puts you "in the zone" at work has the potential to extend your runway as a leader.
  - What kinds of activities in each of your past roles allowed you to slip into a state of flow?
  - As you map out your journey ahead, how can you include more of these types of experiences?
- You regularly use your unique strengths.
  - We feel most fulfilled when we are using our natural talents and strengths.
  - Not sure about your natural aptitudes? Your past can hold clues to your present and future satisfaction:
    - What activities really engaged you as a child?
    - What did you do when you were left entirely to your own devices?
    - What did you excel in?
    - Which of your mental faculties were you using?
    - When were you happiest?
  - If you can't remember, ask the people you grew up with.
  - The insights you learn from this can give you new ideas about what you should be doing tomorrow—and further down your runway.
  - For more objective insights take the StrengthsFinder 2.0, an assessment tool based on Gallup's forty-year study of human strengths. (See Additional Resources section.)
- Most of the stress in your life is positive, rather than negative.
  - Every human life has stress, but not all stress is negative.
  - We experience stress whenever we grow: when we take on a new job, start a new relationship, or learn a new skill.

(continued)

(*continued*)

- As you think about the stress in your life, does it tend to be invigorating and exciting—or damaging and draining?
- If you have negative thoughts about stress, your blood vessels dilate, blood pressure rises, and a range of other physiological consequences can occur.
- If you find stress invigorating and exciting, your blood vessels do not dilate, and your body doesn't suffer any negative consequences.
- Make changes to shift the balance toward positive stress.
- People enjoy being around you.
  - Focus for a moment on the mirror of the people around you. When they interact with you:
    - Do they show that they genuinely like and respect you?
    - Do they give you feedback that they enjoy being around you? Not necessarily verbal feedback, but more like a spark of connection in their eyes.
    - Does their body language convey something positive— either upbeat excitement or a sense of relaxed appreciation?
  - If people don't enjoy being around you, it might be because you are focusing so intently on business achievement that you are not interested in them or are neglecting your own life satisfaction.
- You are free of major regrets.
  - In solitary moments, reflect on:
    - Would I have done something differently in the past?
    - What would I like to do differently in the future?
  - Regularly revisiting and rebalancing your drive for achievement with what you personally value will ensure you can proudly look back on your life twenty years from now without deep regrets.
- ☐ **3. Find a Meaningful Focus**
  - Most hipos have a driving ambition to achieve or create something big. What do you want to accomplish?
  - Reflect for a minute on the focus of your own runway. You don't need to create "the next great thing" like Steve Jobs, but you do need a focus you can commit to—one that inspires you and relates to both your values (what's important to you personally and professionally) and your runway (the ideal path that you want to travel).
  - Write down your focus and reflect on it regularly.
  - If your focus doesn't inspire you or doesn't seem as strong as it needs to be, revise it until it's worth committing to 100 percent.

- If it seems to be too strong—so that it alienates those close to you or interferes with your health and well-being—you may want to temper it by putting a little more focus on increasing satisfaction in your personal life.
- I urge you to avoid the all-too-common trap of losing your health or your closest relationships in search of a career goal that will ultimately bring only fleeting happiness.
- Instead, balance your business focus with your life focus, and continuously look for ideas and opportunities that support them.

☐ **4. Protect Your Mental Health**

- Most of us live with some degree of anxiety about work. We want the self-satisfaction and the rewards that come with accomplishment—and push ourselves hard to achieve it. Mild anxiety is one of the driving forces for almost all high achievers; however—it can take a much more malevolent form, creating a sense of deep apprehension or fear that can be toxic.
- If you start to experience any of the negative physical symptoms of anxiety, such as digestive problems, chest pain, dizziness, high blood pressure, disturbed sleep, loss of appetite, or serious depression, please get professional help immediately. Ignoring the symptoms or keeping a stiff upper lip will only make matters worse.
- When anxiety crosses the line, you're not the only one affected. Anxiety is easily spread, infecting departments, divisions, and even entire companies—not to mention the distress it creates in families.
- It's your job as a leader to create a healthy work environment and to relieve other people's anxiety when it escalates.
- Before you can help others, however, you need to deal with your own anxiety. Watch for the early warning signs in your physical condition or behavior: Are you flying off the handle?
  - Drinking more?
  - Sleeping less?
  - Depending on caffeine or junk food to get you through the day?
- Many leaders are turning to meditation, yoga, exercise, or "power naps" to ease their stress and make them more resilient.
- Seek support from your mentors, friends, and family, or professionals.
- Revisit your work/life balance and be honest, really honest, about whether the job is still right for you.

(continued)

(*continued*)

- If you reach the conclusion that you have to make a major change in your life, remember that the next trajectory is another chance to learn and grow.
- As you learn to healthfully manage your own anxiety, you can start to help reduce the overall anxiety in your team or company. As a leader, you can channel anxiety in productive ways and convert it to positive action:
  - Take a longer-term view of the situation—this helps people see problems in context and reduces anxiety.
  - Engage people in creating solutions to the problems at hand—it gives them a sense of control, which also reduces anxiety.
  - Be honest about the possibilities and risks—if people know that you see the challenges and pitfalls, as well as the opportunities, they will have more trust in your ability to lead them through the challenges to a more positive future.

☐ **5. The Ultimate Practice**
- Devote time each week to reflect on your purpose as a high-potential leader and a human being. A thirty-minute investment (or more) in managing your own potential will bring you extraordinary results.
- Ask yourself the following questions and note any insights in a personal notebook:
  - Are my business achievement and life satisfaction goals in balance?
  - What activities put me "in the zone"—in a state of flow—this week?
  - Did I have plenty of opportunities to use my unique strengths?
  - Did I experience my stress as invigorating and energizing, or draining and debilitating?
  - What have I done this week to increase my ROYT?
  - Did I take any actions to multiply the energy and skills of those around me?
  - Do I have a big idea that I'm excited about now? And have I taken any steps to execute it?
  - What did I learn about my customers, my competitors, and the macro environment?
  - Did I meet any new people I'd like to add to my network this week?
  - What key ideas or insights have I gathered from my reading? My conversations? From any learning events I attended?

- Am I receiving the mentoring I want? If not, what can I do about that?
- Is there anything I need to do to help prepare myself for my next leap?
- You probably won't get answers to every question on the list—and that's fine. Checking off all the boxes is not the goal. Continuing to learn, and grow, and expand your potential in the direction you'd most like to go—that's the goal. Because that's what will help you realize your ultimate sense of purpose as a high-potential leader and a human being.
- Your runway is waiting. I hope you enjoy the journey.

Additional Resources

Kahneman, Daniel. *Thinking, Fast and Slow*. New York: Farrar, Straus and Giroux, 2011.

McGonigal, Kelly. *The Upside of Stress: Why Stress Is Good for You, and How to Get Good at It*. New York: Penguin Publishing Group, 2015.

Rath, Tom. *StrengthsFinder 2.0*. New York: Gallup Press, 2007. (Includes the strengths assessment tool based on Gallup's forty-year study of human strengths.)

Sterner, Thomas. M. *The Practicing Mind: Developing Focus and Discipline in Your Life — Master Any Skill or Challenge by Learning to Love the Process*. Novato, CA: New World Library, 2012.

PART III

THE CARE AND FEEDING OF HIGH POTENTIALS— EVERY ORGANIZATION'S PRECIOUS RESOURCE

9

Identifying, Recruiting, and Retaining Hipos

The train has left the station. At most companies, the journey to transform the company to a digital one has begun. Your role in that journey is to find, recruit, develop, and deploy leaders with high potential to drive the transformation and deftly steer the organization in the emerging context. Be honest about whether you are delivering:

- Does your company have a robust pipeline of leaders with the capabilities needed to meet the *emerging* business challenges?

- Is it head and shoulders above the competition's?

- Are your criteria for identifying high-potential leaders still relevant in light of the changing external landscape?

- Does your company give its hipos opportunities to make big leaps in their development, despite the risks involved?

- Does it deal with the organizational and personal issues associated with accelerating their growth?

Take the initiative to give your company's approach to high-potential leaders a total rethink, starting with four basic principles:

1. **Hipos are a resource for the company, not for an individual boss.** Think of talent as a company resource to be developed, deployed, and assigned in ways that serve the overall interests of the organization. That means bosses can't hoard their high performers, nor block their growth.

2. **Development paths are customized for each individual hipo.** It's no different from what we see happening in the world of consumers, where the customer experience is increasingly customized. With the availability of digital tools to track performance and progress, customized growth plans are not impossible to manage.

3. **The onus is on the individual.** Hipos should be active participants in their development, expected to seek opportunities to make exponential leaps and build their skills.

4. **Growth must be accelerated.** It's in the organization's best interest to help hipos grow as fast as possible. Taking on jobs that would overwhelm others allows them to hone the skills they will need to lead at the highest level. Seven-step career ladders are unnecessary for those who are true hipo leaders and put you at risk of losing them.

Identifying hipos, helping them find and create opportunities to grow exponentially, and continually refreshing the pool should be the central focus of your work.

Redefine and Find High-Potential Leaders

You won't get the leaders you need at high levels if you focus on developing the wrong people. Make the important distinction between hipo leaders and hipo individuals. You need experts with deep knowledge, and the best will earn the respect and admiration of their peers. Some will become de facto leaders in terms of domain knowledge, and some who exhibit leadership traits are well suited to take higher-level jobs in their functional area.

It is rare, however, for the sharpest domain expert to possess the leadership skills required to lead the entire organization. In the first chapter of this book I suggested that hipos do a self-test to decide whether they are truly high-potential leaders. Some people think it is the only path to the highest level of achievement, compensation, and job satisfaction, so they force themselves to fit the mold, even though they fall short in other essential skills such as integrating perspectives from various silos.

HR needs to hold the line to ensure that those identified as hipo *leaders* are chosen because of their *leadership* skills, and not just because they are the smartest, most knowledgeable among their peers. Hipos will perform to a high standard, but they may not be the best technical or functional experts. They're the ones who may be working behind the scenes to help those experts work together to achieve a common goal.

Keep this distinction in sharp focus as you establish the guidelines for identifying hipo leaders. Traits like high integrity and ability to communicate are constants, but others should vary. When I compiled my research on the hipos I'd observed throughout my career, the list of traits was upward of thirty items—too many to apply all at once. A better way to identify hipos is to create a set of minimum criteria they must meet; the skills in this book, for example, are universally important. Then allow for differences, because no two leaders are exactly alike, and no leader is perfect. You'll improve your chances of spotting potential when you create a dialogue among people who know those leaders well. Identifying hipos is essentially a collaboration between senior people and other leaders throughout the company.

Beginning in 2015, CHRO Mary Anne Elliott and CEO Peter Zaffino of Marsh, the insurance brokerage and risk management firm for MMC, revisited the criteria they used to identify hipos, a first step in amping up their efforts to develop and retain them. They were determined to avoid mechanistic checklists, opting instead for an approach that would allow for differences in individuals and in the context. According to Zaffino, "The people we see as having a place in the future of the organization tend to have capabilities in data, analytics, and technology, which fits with our future strategy and the future direction of the business. They also have the ability to engage with people, and to inspire and influence people, even if they're not the direct leaders." Elliott explains, "We don't use a preconceived checklist. It's a matter of looking at a person as a whole package. If you're in Korea versus New York, how you demonstrate leadership is different, or if you're in an emerging business versus a stable one, or in sales versus a finance role."

Zaffino and Elliott were able to identify leaders with different qualities because they made a point of having deep discussions with other leaders in the countries where Marsh operates. It takes time, travel, and attention, but as Elliot says, "When you're in a global environment, you have to get a view of who the hipo is in France, in Johannesburg, and in Chicago, and you have to gather as much information as possible to get it right." Of 4,500 managers and experts, Elliott and Zaffino zeroed in on about 200 they wanted to go to extra lengths to develop and advance. Those identified also were rewarded differently. In addition to their base and bonus compensation, they receive a CEO bonus at the end of the year.

A growing number of companies are using open job market platforms to publicize all positions that are open at the company. These are proving to be an efficient way to match skills and interests with company needs. They can also help you spot hipos. Monitor who is seeking out new and interesting opportunities by applying for jobs that are unexpected next steps.

Google takes an interesting approach to identifying hipo leaders. Laszlo Bock, senior vice president of people operations at Google, says, "The majority of new jobs at Google are individual contributor jobs, and we start with the assumption that we only want incredibly high-potential people. Leadership capability is an essential part of every job, because we want people who will step in and fill a void, then just as easily relinquish power to someone else in a different phase of the problem. We knock people out of the recruiting process for even a tiny signal that they might not function well in a team environment or are not intellectually humble. Then we follow an approach McKinsey & Company is known for, where people get a job title only after they've demonstrated they can do the job."

Create Opportunities for Growth

Hand in hand with rethinking what high-potential leadership looks like, rethink what a hipo's next step ought to be. Hipos need assignments that will test and stretch their capability by thrusting them into unfamiliar territory. There is no substitute for the real thing. While encouraging hipos to take the initiative to define their own paths, you should be helping find or create opportunities for them to make a leap.

In the Bloomberg.com column "How Did I Get Here?" various business leaders describe their paths to the top. It's interesting to note how many steps many of them had to take. Tracey Massey, CEO of Mars Chocolate North America, is typical; I counted seven jobs over twenty-six years, only some of which were leaps. She started in manufacturing, then moved to finance, saying, "I didn't have any experience at all in finance or accounting. I did different jobs and learned everything: payroll, customer collections, planning, control." In this new age, twenty-six years is a long time, and seven steps is too many, especially as companies continue to eliminate hierarchical layers.

If the right openings don't regularly arise, you might have to get creative. Think, for example, about horizontal moves, where the hipo can apply skills at a similar organizational level but in an entirely new geography, function, or business unit.

Remember that hipos will leave if they don't see the chance to progress quickly. You may have to break some taboos to unblock a job that is the best next move for a hipo. Having experienced, competent people stuck in jobs that really need a fresh perspective is a common problem. The incumbent may have been an excellent performer, but in the context of born-digital competitors, the requirements of many jobs are changing. Prepare yourself to make the case that moving people will contribute to repositioning the business and creating value.

Look at changes in organization structure or changes in the definition of a job as an opportunity for a hipo. In August 2016, IBM announced that it was seeking a chief learning officer, which was a new job at the company. A newly created position might mean that no one has the full set of skills required to fill it. Why not put a hipo in that role? Many HR departments are undergoing a kind of transformation as they rethink their role and adopt new tools. A hipo might be a better fit in some HR jobs than those with a traditional HR background. Recognize that a hipo is not likely to stay in those jobs for long. That's okay, because the hipo and the company benefit in the meantime.

Hipos can benefit from being on a team that exposes them to diverse viewpoints and high-level issues. The team will benefit from their wide cognitive bandwidth, their perspective as a consumer, and their comfort with digital technology. Hipos can make useful contributions to strategy discussions, if only by asking incisive questions.

Other kinds of learning experiences are also important. Hindustan Unilever created a program to immerse its management trainees in ambiguous situations, where they had to adapt and deliver results in short order (see Chapter 7). At Marsh, hipos get training opportunities that sometimes include mentorship. In Asia, for example, hipos meet with leaders at the senior vice president level to talk about the industry, local strategy, and career paths, and they get a chance to meet other members of the leadership team. HR tracks all of this.

Coaching is another option that hipos appreciate. Far from the stigma that was attached to coaching a decade ago, having a coach is now considered a "badge of honor" by most leaders. It's an ongoing reminder that the company appreciates them and their contributions and is willing to invest in their success. Whether it's an internal coach from HR or a line of business, or an external coach you've vetted to match company standards, an executive coach can help hipos manage the issues that come from their rapid rise and frequent job changes more effectively. They can also maintain a point of stability as they adapt to new managers more frequently than most employees. Having a consistent person in their corner— someone who knows them well, has their best interests at heart, and understands how to successfully navigate transitions—makes job changes and onboarding easier.

You could encourage hipos to get involved with outside education programs or organizations where similar people get together periodically. The G100, for example, gets CEOs together three times a year to exchange ideas with guest speakers and one another. The individual, not HR, should drive it.

Executive education programs generally provide incremental learning, but they can keep hipos abreast of new tools, new ideas, and new practices, and create an awareness of themselves and others. Over time, that awareness can lead to developmental leaps.

Some programs mix cultural and industry backgrounds, so participants have a chance to expand their frames of reference and build more diverse social networks. In many such programs, the relationships become lifelong. The Harvard Advanced Management Program, for example, assigns group projects months before the attendees arrive on campus. Team members from many countries work virtually before they ever meet face-to-face, and some stay connected long after the program ends.

Some large corporations, notably GE, have well-developed in-house training for their hipos. Hipos benefit most when these programs give them a chance to work on real business problems as part of a cross-functional, cross-business-unit team.

Clear the Path for Hipos

When it comes to selecting people for jobs, HR should be sure that people have the right kind of information about and perspective on hipo candidates. Choosing someone for whom the job is a leap sounds risky, but consider that if the person succeeds, he or she will make an exponential impact on the company. Hipos often create tremendous value.

Be assertive in working with management to create an environment conducive for identifying and growing hipos. You could suggest that talent development be part of the key performance indicators (KPIs) for leaders throughout the company, but that's not enough. Be prepared to address head-on the common issues that arise around accelerating the development of hipos:

> **The boss doesn't want to give them up.** This is conceptually the same thing as a business unit that is generating cash and doesn't want another part of the business to get that money. HR is instrumental here. You can help curb that behavior by creating recognition and incentive programs for business units that export leaders to other units. Remind the leaders who are giving up their talent that they will also be the recipients of talent from other parts of the company.

> **The person doesn't want to move**. Always listen for the reasons. The issue is usually around family and children who don't want to relocate. Maybe a child graduates next year. Some reasons are work-related, such as the hipo who works well with his boss and feels he is still learning from her.

These situations have to be dealt with case by case. Is this move the only way the person can make a leap or develop a new capability? If too many people resist going to a certain location, you may have to think about why. Some companies are headquartered in remote locations, where people are reluctant to move. At some point the company may have to deal with it.

The recipient boss feels he is taking a risk. The recipient boss has to know that part of his job is developing leaders, and managing risk is part of it. He has to have tools to assimilate the person into the existing team. The key here is the speed with which it happens. If the team doesn't stabilize quickly, it will hurt operations. If the process works but assimilation fails, he needs a different person. A receptive boss will be looking for such people and asking for them, rather than resisting.

Improve Feedback Loops

You and your colleagues in HR should take ownership for tracking the progress each hipo is making, and ensuring the accuracy of assessments of how she performed and what she's learned in each new position. The company should have a rhythmic process with a set frequency for high-level people to discuss individual hipos and the hipo gene pool more generally. At least twice a year, you should be asking: Are there enough people in the pool, with the right kinds of leadership skills for the future? An operating system for evaluating hipos is a must, and there are many good examples to follow: Anthem, GE, Bank of America, and Colgate, to name a few.

When it comes to assessing an individual hipo's progress, it's your job to keep it intellectually honest. Insist that line leaders take their hipos seriously by revisiting their progress regularly and by drilling for the specific reasons behind any comments or observations that are being made. Separate the hipo's performance from the context—the things he had no control over or headwinds he faced—and insist on facts. Remember that numbers tell only half the story. Be sure to ask about *how* results were achieved.

Following any move for a hipo that is considered a leap, consider what new skills or traits have become transparent as a result of the experience. Is the person developing a modus operandi to sort out new situations quickly? Did she move fast to build the information networks she needed and to pinpoint the key actions?

This kind of qualitative assessment is not for HR in isolation. Business leaders have to be in the discussion. Time and again I've seen the best insights about people emerge when four or more people share their specific observations simultaneously. That's the best check for filtering out biases.

You can help ensure accuracy by pushing for specific examples to get to the meaning behind people's words. "Strategic thinking," for example, can mean different things to different people. I was present during one such dialogue when four executives were discussing whether a thirty-year-old sales manager could one day be vice president of sales and marketing, and perhaps even CEO. Although the young man was not the highest producer, he had done well in sales. He was a great coach, made good hiring decisions, and built good relationships with customers and colleagues. In the course of the discussion, one of leaders commented on the young man's ability to think strategically. I couldn't help but ask for an example. "Can you tell us something he did to demonstrate that?" I asked. The leader explained that the sales manager had suggested segmenting customers and, for one segment, building a different kind of high-priced sales force that could sell solutions, not just products. Sales to other customers would be handled through the Internet and telephone. It was a great idea that would differentiate the company from the competition.

In a similar conversation at another company, a boss described his protégé as strategic. The evidence? She had changed the incentive scheme to make the sales force more productive. Nobody denied that the change was important, but it was really not strategic.

You can also help by raising dimensions of performance that are important but often missing, such as the ability to get decisions made without having formal authority, and by listening for nuances, positive or negative. Helping hipos develop requires deep understanding of what they can and cannot be expected to do. In one discussion, I heard, "She has incredible potential. She managed the P&L successfully, albeit a small one. She is able to conceive a big idea and is aggressive about it, but when probed in some depth about the details, it makes me quite uncomfortable." Discomfort and inklings like that should not necessarily take a hipo out of the running, but they are something to watch and watch out for, bearing in mind that no leader is perfect.

What should be a disqualifier is if the person is cutting corners and failing to build trust. You may be able to straighten the hipo out if you catch this tendency early, but watch for the greed factor. It will show in asking for high compensation and taking credit for what others did. There's an element of narcissism in it that is psychologically damaging to others. If these people slip through, they may self-destruct later in their careers, as I've seen happen in several cases. They use their guile and intelligence to drive others out and maneuver their way to the top, at a high cost to their personal lives and integrity. Some seek psychotherapy later in life in the wake of horribly damaged family relations. Others end up in jail. In many cases, the telltale signs emerged early. It's HR's job to pick them up.

Digital tools are emerging to help you keep track of hipos—who they are, what they're working on, what developmental leap they need next. But frequent contact and openness to their ideas will go a long way in cementing your relationship with them.

Refresh the Leadership Pool

You should assume that your hipos will be poached, so you'll need to build a recruiting machine to bring in new talent. Allow yourself to get out of the straitjacket of mechanized criteria and traditional recruiting sites and practices to explore other sources of talent. Data analytics can help sort through and find job applicants who don't fit the mold. And some HR leaders are using innovative tools like online contests to find hipos in unexpected places. When they spot talent, they bend the rules to allow those without the usual credentials to get past the filters.

A reputation for accelerating growth helps attract top leadership talent, but gone are the days when you can coast on a big brand name. Many hipos today want to know that they will be contributing to something meaningful. Bock told me what Google's new hires seek: "They want to be doing something that's above and beyond being a market leader or having a cool product. They want to have some kind of meaningful impact. That's true of people in their 40s, 50s, and 60s as well as the younger generation."

Google, of course, is inundated with hipos who want to join its mission of changing the world. But every company should clarify its higher purpose, just as hipos clarify their own. Bock cited the start-up Thumbtack, now a billion-dollar business, as one example: "Jonathan Swanson, one of the founders, started the company because he thought there must be a better way to schedule a plumber, dog walker, personal trainer, and so on. But that's not what attracts people to the company. The pitch to new hires is that the company solves a real problem for small entrepreneurs who are great at doing what they do but not necessarily at running a business. Thumbtack helps those small entrepreneurs live a better life. People feel good about contributing to that mission."

It's easier for high-growth companies or those in turnaround mode, Bock admits, than for companies in the middle to attract hipos looking to make their mark. HR should work with senior management on this.

How to Use This Book to Develop Your Organization's Hipos

Working with the hipos you've identified should be an ongoing, active process, not a bureaucratic one. You should meet with each hipo individually to explain your company's new approach to unleashing his or her potential, emphasizing his or her role in driving his or her personal growth. Remind the hipo that skill building is ongoing, while leaps are periodic. Ask hipos to read this book and decide what capability they want to build and to start thinking about what developmental leaps they might want to make next. The end-of-chapter checklists provide a structured way to develop each skill.

Then meet with the hipo at regular intervals and with his or her boss to discuss progress. Ask for specific examples of where the person has practiced the skill. If you're the CHRO, be sure your colleagues in HR understand the new philosophy and have the training and skill to conduct these discussions.

Use digital tools to track progress, and keep the dialogue going so hipos know they're on your radar. If they are performing well overall, but are struggling with certain aspects of a new role, you can try assigning a mentor, finding a coach with expertise in that area, or suggesting outside educational opportunities.

Remember to keep your own risk aversion in check when hipos reach for bigger opportunities, and let the hipo drive the learning process.

Key Points for Talent Management Leaders

Identifying, Developing, and Building a Pool of Hipos

Companies need talent who can continually reinvent the business to keep it relevant in the complex and fast-changing game.

You play an essential role by building a strong bench of leaders who can not only run the company now but also shape the future.

The following ideas and best practices will help you meet the challenge.

Finding Hipos

- Defining Hipo Criteria

  - Some hipo traits, like high integrity and ability to communicate, are constants, but others should vary.

  - Create a set of minimum criteria every hipo must meet, and then allow for individual differences, because leadership differs depending on the context.

  - Collaborate with senior executives and other leaders throughout the company to spot leadership talent.

  - Be sure your criteria differentiate between hipo *leaders* and hipo *individuals*—your goal is to select the company's future leaders, not the great solo performers who have no capacity for leadership.

- Selecting Internal Hipos

  - Hipos are the lifeblood of your leadership pipeline, so it pays to be assertive in working with management to identify and grow hipo leaders.

  - Strongly suggest that talent development be part of the KPIs for leaders throughout the company, and reward managers for identifying them.

  - Meet individually with business leaders once or twice a year.

  - Ask about their growth areas and needs for high-potential talent.

  - Discuss who they see as having high potential to lead and how they will develop them.

- Work with them on development plans for the hipos in their group.

- Spot hipos by watching for those who seek new challenges and apply for unexpected next steps in the open job market.

- Build an operating system for evaluating hipos using good examples from companies such as Anthem, GE, Bank of America, and Colgate.

- Create an annual or semiannual dialogue among managers and senior leaders who know the hipo candidates well. The best insights about a person's talent emerge when four or more people share their specific observations simultaneously.

- Once identified, let the hipo know that she or he is believed to have high potential.

  - Meet with each hipo individually to explain your company's approach to unleashing his or her potential, emphasizing his or her role in driving his or her own personal growth.

  - Remind the hipo that skill building is ongoing, while leaps are periodic.

  - Ask hipos to read this book and decide what *capability* they want to build and to start thinking about what *developmental leap* they might want to make next.

  - The end-of-chapter checklists provide a structured way to develop each skill.

- Hiring External Hipos

  - If your company has a reputation for attracting great people and accelerating leaders' growth, you will naturally attract other hipos. But you have to assume that some of your hipos will be poached, so it's wise to build an innovative recruiting machine to bring in new talent.

- Get out of the straitjacket of mechanized criteria and traditional recruiting sites and practices to explore other sources of talent.

- Some HR leaders are using innovative tools like online contests to find hipos in unexpected places.

- When you need to use traditional recruiting sites, use untraditional job criteria and data analytics to help sort through and find job applicants who don't fall into the usual linear growth patterns.

- Look for people who have successfully taken big leaps, who learn quickly, who have been effective in very different roles or fields, or who have rapidly progressed within a single company.

- If someone's résumé shows rapid progression, but it's across multiple companies with short tenure in each role, check references carefully. This could be a sign of a large ego or greed combined with a high level of charisma, rather than a sign of true talent.

- When you spot true talent, be willing to bend the rules to allow those without the usual credentials to get past the filters.

Developing Hipos

- Internal Development Opportunities

  - If you have a corporate university or other internal training options, consider developing a program to meet the specific needs of hipos.

- Hipos benefit most when these programs give them a chance to work on real business problems as part of a cross-functional, cross-business-unit team—especially when sponsored by a senior executive who can add to their learning.

- Consider offering hipos a role in a newly formed task force or volunteer opportunity that exposes them to diverse viewpoints and high-level issues.

- Set up a unique event that's just for hipos so they can meet and interact with their peers. In one Asian company, hipos meet with leaders at the senior vice president level to talk about the industry, local strategy, and career paths, and they get a chance to meet other members of the leadership team.

- Some companies offer mentorships with senior leaders. Formal mentoring programs can be tricky to get right, but when a good match is made it can be invaluable for fostering a hipo's learning and loyalty to the company.

- Coaching is another option that hipos appreciate and it's especially helpful during onboarding and job transitions.

- External Development Opportunities

  - Encourage hipos to get involved with outside education programs, attend conferences or industry events, and explore online learning options.

  - Executive education programs generally provide incremental learning, but they can keep hipos abreast of new tools, new ideas, and new practices and create awareness of oneself and others. They can also help fill in knowledge gaps to support a hipo's next big leap.

- Some programs mix cultural and industry backgrounds so participants have a chance to expand their frames of reference and build diverse social networks.

- When they return to work after a program, have them share what they learned with their managers, teams, and others. This not only deepens their own learning but also gets them in the habit of developing others.

- Hipos should drive their own learning, and Chapter 6 of this book provides a range of options to guide them in doing that.

- Other excellent development options can be found in the book *Global Leadership: The Next Generation*, by Marshall Goldsmith et al., listed in the Additional Resources section at the end of this chapter.

Accelerating Hipos' Growth

- Managing Their Runways

- Rethink your job to support hipos as they pursue their own fast growth.

- Hipos need assignments that will test and stretch their capability by thrusting them into unfamiliar territory. They are highly motivated by tough challenges and grow restless and bored if their learning slows.

- A growing number of companies are using open job market platforms to publicize all internal positions that are vacant. If your company has this resource, your hipos can use it to search for their next jobs.

- While encouraging hipos to take the initiative to define their own paths, you should also help find or create opportunities for them to make leaps.

- Remember that hipos will leave if they don't see the chance to progress quickly.

- If good openings don't regularly arise, you might have to get creative.

- Think about horizontal moves, where the hipo can apply skills at a similar organizational level but in an entirely new geography, function, or business unit.

- Look at changes in organization structure or changes in the definition of a job as an opportunity for a hipo.

- Put them on a task force or ad hoc project that keeps them learning and growing.

- If you find a good opportunity but the hipo doesn't want to move, dig deeper to find out why:

  - Is it a family that doesn't want to relocate, a strong loyalty to the current boss, or something else? Each case is unique and needs to be considered individually to see if there's a way to ease the resistance.

  - If the resistance is because of the location, and other people have refused to go there, too, you may have to think about why—and what you can do to improve the environment there.

  - If the reason for their resistance is unshakable, explore other options. Is this move the only way the person can make a leap or develop a new capability? What other growth areas can you find?

- Some hipos may push for a new leap before they've been successful in their current situation. If so, remind them that they need to tackle their current challenges first. Brainstorm ideas that could help them expand their knowledge and skills or improve their relationships and networks. When they've mastered their current challenges they will be ready to leap.

- There may be times when you need to consider removing someone from your hipo list:

  - One disqualifier is if the person is cutting corners and failing to build trust. You may be able to straighten the hipo out if you catch this tendency early.

  - A more serious disqualifier is the greed factor. It will show in asking for high compensation, taking credit for what others did, and focusing more on the job's title and prestige than on the learning opportunities. This is a personality issue and is unlikely to change. Cut your losses and remove the person from your hipo list.

- Managing Their Managers

  - There's no greater influence on a hipo—whether positive or negative—than his or her manager, so it's important for you to manage the manager as well as the hipo.

  - If talent development is part of the KPIs for leaders throughout the company, you're likely to have a willing accomplice in managing the hipo's growth, especially if the competency of "developing others" is tied to the manager's compensation in some way.

  - If talent development isn't one of the manager's KPIs, be prepared to address head-on two of the common challenges that arise around accelerating the development of hipos:

- Challenge 1: The current boss doesn't want to give them up.

  - You can help curb that behavior by creating recognition and incentive programs for business units that export leaders to other units.

  - Assure the leaders who are giving up their talent that they will also be the recipients of top talent from other parts of the company.

- Challenge 2: The recipient boss feels the move is a risk.

  - Remind recipient bosses that developing talent is part of their job, and managing the risks associated with that is one of their own development tasks as leaders.

  - Ensure that the boss has the knowledge and tools to effectively onboard the person and assimilate the hipo into the existing team. Provide articles, guidelines, or your personal guidance as needed.

  - A transition coach can help the hipo get up to speed more quickly so that the unit's productivity doesn't suffer. The coach can also help the manager become more effective in managing the new team dynamics.

  - If the process works but the person fails, find the manager a new person quickly.

- Insist that line leaders take their hipos seriously by revisiting their progress regularly and reminding them of the essential role they play in developing the company's future leaders.

Monitoring Hipos

- Monitoring the Hipo Pool

  - You and your colleagues in HR should take ownership for tracking the progress each hipo is making. Ensure that performance assessments are accurate and document what's been learned in each new position.

  - If you're the CHRO, be sure your colleagues in HR understand the company's hipo philosophy and have the training and skill to manage the responsibilities well.

  - Establish a rhythmic process with a set frequency for high-level people to discuss individual hipos and the hipo gene pool more generally. At least twice a year, you should be asking:

    - Are there enough people in the pool?

    - Do they have the right kinds of leadership skills for the future?

    - Is the pool populated with hipo *leaders* rather than hipo *individuals*? You want a cadre of people who can lead, motivate, engage, and inspire others to fill your leadership pipeline.

  - A growing number of digital platforms and tools can help not just with hiring but also with developing, managing, and retaining your hipos. They make it easier to track an individual hipo's growth and can also help you assess and report on the overall health of your hipo pool.

  - Monitor platforms such as Glassdoor to learn what your employees have to say about their job satisfaction.

This can influence a hipo's willingness to join your firm and either hurt or help in your recruiting process.

- Improve feedback loops between hipos and their managers—and track the quality and frequency of feedback. Hipos in particular need frequent feedback on:

  - What they are doing well

  - What they can improve on, and

  - How they can grow quickly.

- Many companies with leading HR practices are now implementing manager feedback sessions on a monthly or biweekly basis or as part of weekly manager check-in meetings.

- Monitoring the Individual Hipos

  - The new digital tools can help you keep track of individual hipos—who they are, what they're working on, and what developmental leaps they need next—but be sure you also include regular personal touch points.

  - Keep a steady dialogue going so hipos know they're on your radar and that you care about their development. Frequent contact and openness to their ideas will go a long way in cementing the relationship.

  - Meet with their managers at regular intervals:

    - Ask for the manager's feedback on the hipo, and drill down for the specific reasons behind any comments or observations.

    - How well are they managing the responsibilities of their new roles?

    - What new skills have they learned?

- What new traits have become transparent?

- What new ideas have they come up with—and implemented?

- How well are they managing their new relationships?

- Separate the hipo's performance from the context— the things he or she had no control over or headwinds he faced, and insist on facts rather than opinions.

- If the hipo is performing well overall, but struggling with certain aspects of a new role, ask whether the manager thinks the situation could be improved by assigning an internal mentor, a coach with expertise in the area, or an outside educational opportunity.

- Remember that numbers tell only half the story. Be sure to ask about the hipo's leadership style and how results were achieved.

- It's important to monitor a hipo more closely for a while following any move that is considered a leap.

  - Check in briefly with his manager, peers, and teams. It doesn't take much time; just a short phone call or e-mail can give you the information you need to make any quick interventions needed to keep the hipo on track.

    - Is the person developing a modus operandi to sort out new situations quickly?

    - Did she quickly build the networks to get the information she needed and pinpoint the key actions?

    - What is one thing he could do to be more effective?

Top Three Actions You Can Take

If time is short and you can only implement a few of these practices, here are the three I recommend:

1. Ensure that your selection criteria differentiate between hipo *leaders* and hipo *individuals*. Don't try to shoehorn great technicians who have no capacity for leadership into managerial roles. And don't use long checklists as filters. Instead, allow for unique combinations of leadership traits.
2. Make sure your hipos have opportunities to make big leaps in their development; otherwise they will seek learning and growth elsewhere. Track their emerging skills and talents along with their performance.
3. Put the onus on the hipos to set a customized path, but help clear the way for your hipos' exponential growth.

Additional Resources

Charan, Ram, Stephen Drotter, and James Noel. *The Leadership Pipeline: How to Build the Leadership Powered Company.* San Francisco, CA: John Wiley & Sons, Inc., 2011.

Conaty, Bill, and Ram Charan. *The Talent Masters: Why Smart Leaders Put People Before Numbers.* New York: Crown Publishing Group, 2010.

Goldsmith, Marshall, et al. *Global Leadership: The Next Generation.* Upper Saddle River, NJ: Pearson Education, Inc., 2003.

Lund, Susan, James Manyika, and Kelsey Robinson. "Managing Talent in a Digital Age." *McKinsey Quarterly*, March 2016.

Acknowledgments

This book began one day when I was teaching a newly designed program for high-potential leaders at Wharton Business School. Deb Giffen, director of Innovative Learning Solutions at Wharton Executive Education, inspired me to create a book with practical hands-on advice aimed at the new generation of leaders. I agreed to try to fill the void if she would lend her expertise. Her broad-based knowledge of leadership concepts and best practices and her ability to translate ideas into practical tools is unsurpassed. I am deeply grateful for her substantive contributions, especially for doing the heavy lifting in creating the checklists.

What really brings this book to life are the firsthand accounts that many busy and accomplished leaders so generously shared with me. I am grateful beyond words for their willingness to tell their stories and share their learning. In particular, I want to thank Dom Barton, Kishore Biyani, Laszlo Bock, Dennis Carey, Mike DeDomenico, Love Goel, Mary Anne Elliott, Mark Fields, Pat Gallagher, Kiran Kumar Grandhi, Aaron Greenblatt, Deb Henretta, Bonnie Hill, Aaron Levie, Sunil Mittal, Tony Palmer, Ivan Seidenberg, Ning Tang, Tadashi Yanai, and Peter Zaffino.

I have learned from many other thinkers and leaders over the years, including: Dick Antoine, Gene Batchelder, Cathy Benko, John Berisford, Bruce Broussard, John Chiminski, Bill Conaty, Ian Cooke, Roger Cude, Frank D'Souza, Alex Gorsky, Fred Hassan,

Chad Holliday, Tim Huval, Andrea Jung, P.M. Kumar, A.G. Lafley, John Luke, Gracia Martore, Santrup Misra, Alan Mulally, Jim Mulva, Doug Petersen, Sajan Pillai, Kevin Plank, Brent Saunders, Matt Smith, Mary Szela, Kathy Wallace, Hou Weigui, and Julia Yang.

Geri Willigan, who has collaborated with me for the past twenty-three years, gave order to the many ideas and bits of information she fielded and captured them in clear, direct language. As always, I am appreciative of her ability to draw the best out of me and "talk" to the reader.

Thank you to Charlie Burck, who used his superb editorial skills to get this book started, and to Mark Esher-Hagel who provided useful feedback in a later stage. Thanks also to my editor, Richard Narramore, who patiently guided me to shape the content in the best interests of the target audience, and to Tiffany Colon and the rest of the Wiley team for their flexibility and hard work in taking this book across the finish line.

My work life would not have stayed on track for a single day without the immensely competent support I receive from Cynthia Burr and Jodi Engleson. I am thankful to have their help daily.

Last, I am greatly encouraged by the leadership talent I see in the world and am grateful for the next generation's vision, dedication, and desire to make a positive impact on the world. We will all benefit from their growth.

Index